SHE ROARED in CLASSROOM 250

Sterling N. Sorrell

Alice Elizabeth Nye Sorrell

SHE ROARED in CLASSROOM 250

Sterling N. Sorrell

A Memoir

East of the Mountains  and West of the Sun

RHYOLITE PRESS LLC
Colorado Springs, Colorado

Copyright © 2020 Sterling N. Sorrell

All Rights Reserved. No portion of this book may be reproduced in any form or by any electronic or mechanical means, including information storage and retrieval systems, without permission from the publisher, except by a reviewer who may quote brief passages in a review.

Published in the United States of America by Rhyolite Press LLC
P.O. Box 60144
Colorado Springs, Colorado 80960
www.rhyolitepress.com

She Roared in Classroom 250
Sterling N. Sorrell

First edition: July 1, 2020

Library of Congress Control Number: 2020909317
ISBN 978-0-9839952-5-8

Publisher's Cataloging-in-Publication Data

Names: Sorrell, Sterling N., author.

Title: She roared in classroom 250 : the story of Alice Elizabeth Nye Sorrell / Sterling N. Sorrell.

Description: From cover: "A story of family , perseverance , and education." | Includes bibliographical references. | Colorado Springs, CO: Rhyolite Press, 2020.

Identifiers: LCCN: 2020909317 | ISBN: 9780983995258

Subjects: LCSH Sorrell, Alice Elizabeth Nye. | Sorrell, Alice Elizabeth Nye--Family. | Educators--Texas--Biography. | Journalists--Texas--Biography. | Women--Texas--Biography. | BISAC BIOGRAPHY & AUTOBIOGRAPHY / Educators

Classification: LCC LA2317.S639 .S67 2020 | DDC 371.1/0092--dc23

PRINTED IN THE UNITED STATES OF AMERICA

Cover and book design/layout by Donald R. Kallaus

She Roared in Classroom 250 was written to honor the soul and spirit of Alice Elizabeth Nye Sorrell, deceased. But the story and its message are dedicated as well to her grandchildren, Andrew N. Sorrell, of Blanco, Texas, and Virginia Elizabeth Lynn, a resident of Madison, Alabama, and to Alice Elizabeth's eight great-grandchildren in Texas and Alabama.

—Done this 15th of October in the year of Our Lord, 2019
   Sterling N. Sorrell

TABLE OF CONTENTS

Prologue	xi
GHOSTS IN THE ATTIC	1
A NORSE CLAN CALLED "NYE"	5
VOYAGE TO THE NEW WORLD	15
GENETICS AS DESTINY	29
THE ORPHAN AND PROTECTED PERSON	33
FAMILY FERMENT	41
MEN OF GERMAN DESCENT	53
SOCIETY BETWEEN SAN ANTONIO AND MEXICO	61
RAYMOND & TIRZA MARTIN HIGH SCHOOL–1937	69
STRUGGLE AND FAMILY ANECDOTES	75
THE WAR'S IMPACT	81
EMPTY NEST–1955	87
ELIZABETH'S ALLOTTED TIME FROM 1989-2006	91
Epilogue	97
Acknowledgments	101
Appendices:	
Her Final Fiesta, Obituary, Letter interpretation, Transcription	103
Notes /Bibliography	115

PROLOGUE

Definition: An introduction to a poem, play, etc.; esp. introductory lines spoken by a member of the cast before a dramatic performance. Also: a preliminary act or course of action foreshadowing greater events.
— Webster's New World College Dictionary, 3rd Ed. Copyright, 1997, 1996, 1994, 1991, 1998 by Simon & Schuster, Inc.

The January 9, 2007, *San Antonio Express News* published a piece entitled "A remarkable life" about Elizabeth Nye Sorrell, then a resident at The Meadows assisted living facility for elderly situated on Babcock Road. Wrote staff writer Melissa Fletcher Stoeltje:

"She's about to turn 98 and she's still working on deadline. Meet the remarkable Elizabeth Nye Sorrell, a woman who defies notions about what it means to grow old, a former longtime teacher and newspaper columnist who has touched the lives of legions of South Texans—and continues to do so with her voracious curiosity and lust for life."

A photo of Alice Elizabeth Sorrell, nee Nye, born in Laredo at the Nye family onion farm in February 1909, overshadows Ms. Stoeltje's lede. It shows Alice Elizabeth Nye Sorrell as a pre-teen girl smiling directly into the camera, sporting a prince valiant haircut, dark in color, her left forearm and fingers propped just under her chin, white dress and stockings reflecting the lighting of the posed picture.

She was less than twelve years of age when the portrait was made in Laredo, TX, so the year of the photo session was earlier than February of 1921. Her grandfather, Thomas C. Nye, born in 1844 at Matagorda, in the Texas Republic, had died in Laredo in August 1917, at Nye Station along the rail siding where farmed onions were packed for shipment northward. The child's mother, Faye McCluskey, resided in the Nye Family homestead in Laredo, but was entering a state of disability with arthritis.

Ms. Stoeltje's story preceded Alice Elizabeth Nye's death by seven months. Several towering personalities who participated in her funeral in Laredo, insisted that *someone* "must" collect her books, papers, and family history lore to prepare a biography, to be published undoubtedly by some university or college press in Texas. It fell to the lady's sole surviving son to gather the material and prepare for publication by founding *An Archive of Elizabeth Nye Sorrell, MA, LLC*, in Colorado.

Here is the *San Antonio Express-News* interview with Alice Elizabeth Sorrell at The Meadows assisted living facility in its entirety:

A remarkable life

Soon to be 98, writer, former teacher still going strong

By Melissa Fletcher Stoeltje
EXPRESS-NEWS STAFF WRITER

She's about to turn 98 and she's still working on deadline.

Meet the remarkable Elizabeth Nye Sorrell, a woman who defies notions about what it means to grow old, a former longtime teacher and newspaper columnist who has touched the lives of legions of South Texans — and continues to do so with her voracious curiosity and lust for life.

She would be embarrassed by such accolades, no doubt. Charming and self-effacing, Sorrell insists she's only ordinary. But what ordinary 97-year-old would still be hard at work on three different stories for a small publication in her native Laredo, profiles of three Laredoans she will tap out on the typewriter at the Meadows Retirement Community on Babcock Road, her home for the last four years?

When she's not writing stories, she's firing off letters to the editor of the newspaper, which she devours every day.

Former students are forever visiting her and sending her correspondence, still entranced by the mentor who shaped their attitudes toward literature. Such was the man who recently stopped by to give Sorrell a copy of the book he'd just published. "To the greatest English teacher in the universe," he wrote inside the cover.

"Whether it's in terms of her knowledge of politics or culture or her vital interest in the world, she's a role model for everybody," says the poet Naomi Shihab Nye, whose husband is a distant cousin to Sorrell. "She's a real activist and always has been."

Nye had never met Sorrell before, didn't even know they were distantly related. Then one day an "amazing, beautifully eloquent" letter, written in gorgeous longhand, landed in Nye's mailbox. It was Sorrell's impassioned support for an editorial Nye had recently published in the Express-News critical of the Iraq war, which at that time was ramping up. Nye knew she had to meet her fan.

"We sat there in the lobby (of the Meadows) discussing politics," she recalls. "It was so fantastic to meet someone so outspoken and so will-

See TEACHER/4C

CONTINUED FROM 1C

ing to put her views and feelings on the table."

On a recent morning Sorrell took a break from traveling around the Meadows with her walker to talk about her long and storied life, which began on an onion farm in Laredo on Feb. 4, 1909. Incredibly healthy — the heart and blood pressure medicines she takes are merely preventive — she is also articulate and funny, if a tad hard of hearing. She has pillowy white hair and wears a purple brocade dress and wire-frame glasses. At one point in the conversation she launches into a recitation from memory of the witch's poem from "Macbeth."

"You know the talk about 'fair is foul and foul is fair' is the theme of 'Macbeth,'" she says, slipping into English teacher mode. "It's about the conflict between good and evil."

Sorrell's story has burnished roots. Her ancestors came over on the ship directly after the Mayflower. Her great-grandfather traveled from Massachusetts to Matagorda and then perished in a hurricane. His son, Thomas C. Nye — Sorrell's beloved grandfather — fought for the Confederacy and was captured in the Civil War. He escaped and went on to become the "Onion King of the Rio Grande," being the first to plant that crop in the irrigated Laredo soil.

It was on her grandfather's lap that Sorrell acquired her love of learning and reading. "I first learned the word 'book' from him," she says.

Her own father was a prosperous onion farmer, too, until she turned 3 and they moved into the big city of Laredo. Her father died when she was young, and ultimately the land had to be sold. But Sorrell inherited the strong work ethic of her ancestors and began working for the local newspaper when she was in high school, covering football games for 10 cents a published column inch.

After graduating from high school in 1927, Sorrell attended Rice University in Houston, living with an aunt and uncle and working the switchboard at Methodist Hospital to help pay for her education. (Her mother, an invalid, died while she was in college.)

NICOLE FRUGÉ/STAFF

Elizabeth Nye Sorrell taught English for decades and turned her home into a literary salon.

After graduating from Rice in 1931, she returned home to Laredo and began teaching math at the local high school until an opening arose in the English department, her real love. She married and had one child, Sterling Sorrell Jr., now 68, and a lawyer in Colorado. Her husband, Sterling Norman Sorrell, who worked in a tax office, died of a heart attack when she was just 33. Sorrell never remarried.

Her life has been full, however. In addition to teaching, Sorrell turned her home into the equivalent of a literary salon, where students would come to read poetry, sing and have intellectual discussions. She later earned a master's in English from the University of Texas at Austin.

Sheila Glassford, 72, is a former student in Laredo and an old friend of Sorrell who talks to her by phone every week. She recalls how her old mentor would turn an everyday class on Shakespeare into something special.

"She would read 'MacBeth' to us, and we would all sit with bated breath until she reached the line, 'Out, out damn spot!'" says Glassford. "Oh, my gosh, she had such a tremendous voice, so theatrical. It's like she could have been onstage."

In addition to teaching, Sorrell for decades wrote a well-loved social column, first for the South Texas Citizen and later for the Laredo Morning Times. She also wrote observational columns. People far and wide knew who she was and avidly followed her writing. In her Meadows apartment, on a wall lined with plaques and teaching awards, there is a government proclamation honoring "Lines from Liz," the name of her column.

She retired from teaching at age 70; she kept up with the newspaper writing until she turned 85. Sorrell says the three profiles she's currently working on for LareDos (for no pay; two of them are on former students) will be her last. "I've had enough," she says. "They want people from Laredo, and I've run out of people."

Sorrell, who has two grandchildren and four great-grandchildren, moved to San Antonio from Laredo at age 94, first to live with a granddaughter and then to move into her present abode. She is saddened by the state of things in her old hometown — the drug cartels, the violence. No, she never goes back. And she is not at all averse to stating her opinion about the current occupant of the White House.

"I don't like Bush at all. I think he's awful," she says. "He told lies about Iraq, and I don't think we should have gone in there at all. I don't believe in spilling American blood on things like that. I don't think the world has ever looked as bad as it does now."

But mostly her days are filled with peace and light. She loves venturing around the complex with her walker, admiring the squirrels and the birds. At her suggestion, the retirement community instituted its own reading series, where people recite poems and prose. Sorrell can see both the "sunrise and the moonrise" from her fourth-story apartment, and there's plenty of "star shine" as well. She knows the full names of all her peers at the complex and — like a true journalist — she knows all their life stories.

Her doctor has told her he thinks she's going to live to see 100.

"I don't have the secret to living so long," she responds, when asked. "I'm just thankful that I'm here. But I don't mind the idea of death, either. I am resigned to the fact that we all have to go."

But what a life it's been.

stoeltje@express-news.net

What follows this Prologue is an attempt to relate the "back story" of a Norse clan which, starting in Denmark and England, dispersed Nye descendants to Cape Cod, Massachusetts, with a follow-on migration to the Texas Gulf coast. Then ultimately, to the U.S.-Mexico borderland. With bells, whistles and poetry the American Nye generation fielded Alice Elizabeth for a ninety-eight-year "run" as English lit teacher, for fifty years and an outspoken journalist, culture chronicler, and raconteur of the Texas scene for nearly nine decades!

Imagine, if you will, a sword-wielding replica of Boadicea gob smacking the likes of *both* George W. Bush and Donald Trump? What fun, with poetry and song thrown into the mix, as well.

Nurture of Alice Elizabeth

An uncle by marriage, Everett Shipplett, a native of Illinois, had served in World War I. He was able to support his wife, Inez, the two Nye nieces and little Miles Nye because he was gainfully employed in Houston during the years surrounding the Wall Street market collapse in 1929.

Aunt Inez and Uncle Everett had no children of their own. After the deaths of Captain T. C. Nye in 1917 and Faye McCluskey Nye in Laredo in 1928, the family homestead on Farragut Street was rented due to hospitalization of A. P. Nye and removal of his three children to the care of their Aunt Inez, in Houston, after about 1926, when Elizabeth graduated from Old High.

Practically all we have been saying is the result of research in the years since 1952 and later during the retirement of Alice Elizabeth Nye and by our mining the archival information contained in family correspondence, newspaper clippings, and anecdotal accounts of Nye family history from many Laredo or family sources, all of which have been in the Archive of Elizabeth Nye Sorrell, gathered at the time of her death in San Antonio, Texas in July 2007. Elizabeth had compiled many letters, books, and records after her retirement from teaching that we are in possession of now.

"American Nyes of English origin"

The data presented in this biography of Alice Elizabeth Nye Sorrell, concerning and identifying several descendants of Benjamin Nye, born in England before 1636, is based upon the works compiled by L. Bert Nye, Jr., first published in November 1977 (Volume I) and which was augmented by Vol. II, in November 1990.[1]

Mr. L. Bert Nye's work was carried on under auspices of the Nye Family of America Association of East Sandwich, MA, and entitled, *A Genealogy of American Nyes of English Origin* (Volumes I and II). No quotation of the entries in such works is included here. The author of this book has referred extensively here to the Nye geneaology compilations, the L. Bert Nye, Jr. works, by end-notes in which we distinguish between Vol. I and Vol, II, where needed, in order to identify specific descendants who are ancestors of Alice Elizabeth Nye Sorrell, mentioned throughout this biographical writing. The scope of Vol. I covers generations one through eight, and Vol. II covers generations nine through twelve. From time to time we will refer to the genealogy as "Gen 8, Vol. I, p____," for generations eight or earlier, and where the descendant identified is a part of generation nine or later, the reference will be "Gen 9 Vol. I, p___."

Elizabeth's grandfather, Thomas Carter Nye, b. May 17, 1844 (whose wife was Grandmother Frances Elizabeth Shultz), was in the seventh generation of Benjamin Nye descendants, identified at p. 440 of Vol. I, or therefore, "Gen 7, Vol. I, p. 440."

After study, research, and anecdotal observances over the years since about 1944, this author has developed a hypothesis about the traits and actions of the descendants of Benjamin Nye after 1636: They acted out, lived out, and demonstrated by their lives the cultural and genetic heritages that came to each Nye generation—down from English as well as Norse and Danish progenitors who had invaded England before 1000 A.D. The invaders did not "declare victory" and go to homes on the continent, but stayed to intermarry with men and women of Saxon clans native to the island long prior to 1000 A.D.

Therefore, the biography of an independent woman born in Texas in 1909 is enriched by the insertion of material that can be partially "proved" by genomic science and microbiology that is new and has surfaced in the fields of archaeology (and anthropology) since the mid-twentieth century.

Why would a biographer of Elizabeth Nye, b. 1909 at Laredo, Webb County, TX, look as far back as England in 1620 to 1635 to locate a reason or motive for Benjamin Nye's embarkation on the ship *Abigail* at Plymouth, England, with about 200 other souls whose purpose was to emigrate forever out of their homeland in England? As we have heard from the original English colonization stories, many, perhaps most, anticipated wars, rebellions, and persecution by the established church in England, under, among other kings, Charles I, who as an adherent of the Roman Catholic Church sought to discourage "dissenters" by various means.

The Nyes in the area South of London—Kent, for example, had among them people who had fled to Holland, and some even returned to England, only to continue their search for freedom from oppression and for greener pastures in the New World, where they hoped to enjoy independent control of their livelihood and destiny.

It was history repeating itself. A few hundred years earlier, Nye clans from northern Europe had migrated to (invaded?) England west over sea—also to "start over" and to escape circumstances not sufficiently under their control.

One objective of this biography of my mother, Elizabeth Nye Sorrell, is to encourage other Nye descendants in Texas to compile histories of their families after World War II for submission for a new volume of Nye family history to the Nye Family of America Association, of East Sandwich, MA, covering the ongoing work of descendants from Benjamin Nye in 1640 and their blending with other families in Mexico or Europe who melded together beginning in or about the founding of the Republic of Texas since 1840.

I cannot imagine a more colorful and inspiring story of immigration from Northern Europe, combining with other migrant fortune seekers whose paths collided at the Rio Bravo Del Norte. This was shortly after the founding of Laredo by Don Tomas Sanchez on the north bank of the river, which was one hundred years earlier than the Republic of Texas. As they met (peacefully) and lived side by side for the century and a half after 1840, these families became neighbors, they socialized, they went to the same churches and schools, they went on to the same universities and colleges, and they intermarried, blending into an amalgamated culture that is now well established on both sides of the Rio Grande River.

It confounded many of us in 2015 –'16 who have lived on both sides of the border to hear a crude Anglo "maverick" political figure, born in Brooklyn, New York, display his ignorance, stigmatizing so many of us who are descended from blended-culture families, native to that huge scape of lands lying west of the Sabine River (East Texas), which roll on into deserts, mountains, and farms as far as San Diego, Southern California's coast on the Pacific Ocean.

Many who read this biography of a Rice University graduate who taught and wrote for so many decades will recognize that her story, nascent in England and New England, then bore a vital, flowering, fruitful harvest in Laredo public schools—especially Raymond and Tirza Martin High School—and in literary and news journalism communities all over south Texas, including San Antonio.

The harvest is seen in thousands of households enjoying blessed liberty and "fraternity" in peace and prosperity, which continues to burgeon like yeast for bread (or "water for chocolate") and in *masa de harina o masa de maiz* (dough of the flour or dough of the corn). The harvest for Elizabeth is seeing both love and joy in the culture increase exponentially during her productive life. Friends still feel her presence, overlooking God's creatures in our world, celebrating with poems in the cirrus and cumulus clouds written by Chaucer and the Bard—plus Cervantes, Willie Morris, and even the likes of Leonard Cohen!

Elizabeth's memoir was begun in 2016—107 years after her birth to Faye McCluskey Nye, in Laredo. A writer always asks, "Where shall I begin?" You say, "Of course, begin at the beginning!" At least nominally, Alice Elizabeth Nye would have accepted the real beginning: Genesis 1:1: "In the beginning God created the heaven and the earth . . ." And, perhaps, Gen. 1:26: "Let us make man in our image, after our likeness . . ." Then Gen. 1:27: "So God created man in his own image, in the image of God created he them; male and female . . . and God said to them, be fruitful, and multiply and replenish the earth, and subdue it . . ."

Her mother and grandparents had fostered a tradition of Christian faith out of which the parents and grandparents had sprung forth in and around Matagorda, TX, on the Gulf Coast, beginning in 1840, when Thomas Carter Nye and a sibling were left orphans. They were infants less than a year old, when the local Anglican parish church, Christ Church, saw to it that these two orphan boys were taken in by a guardian who brought them up as church community children and young adults.

GHOSTS IN THE ATTIC

The old house had many quirks and curiosities in its construction—high ceilings, old gas light fixtures that had been wired for electricity when power became available in the years around World War I. Then there was the cellar, running the width of the house under the rear kitchen, bath and the so-called "back apartment" that was rented to the Army Air Corps sergeants during World War II, 1944-1946.

Young Sterling Sorrell was attended by a *criada* (maid) during the daytime hours when Elizabeth was at Martin High School, during her classroom teaching day. He explored the cellar, enclosed in a brick foundation dating back to the last decade of the nineteenth century, when a banker named Barrera was reputed to have built the house. Then there was the attic with a "widows walk" centered in the wood shingle roof with a pitch of about thirty degrees, a rare design for the semi-arid weather of Laredo. The attic was huge, and, with high ceilings on the main floor, afforded relief from summer heat, along with the curved veranda elevated four feet above the grade of the house lot.

Tall French windows and doors along the brick walls of the east and south verandas could be opened to the shaded exterior of the veranda. Breezes from the Gulf of Mexico 150 miles to the east further gave Alice Elizabeth, her family, and old Capt. Thomas C. Nye cool comfort on the warmest evenings in the summer or fall.

No one ever lowered the wood ladder stairway recessed in the ceiling of the hallway that led up into the attic. Nothing presumably was stored in the attic space. Word was that the floor of the attic space was covered with gray dust nearly an inch thick, and one couldn't walk up there without becoming covered in dust blown in through old wood shingles. Eventually–maybe 1949 or 1950–little Sterling managed to untie the rope from woodwork in the rear hallway and lowered the stairway leading to the attic. It took some nerve to climb the ladder, overcoming the vertigo that came on about twelve feet above the hallway floor. No word of the discovery in the attic was spoken to any adult down below in the house, where the clatter of dish washing by hand came from a kitchen far from the front hallway.

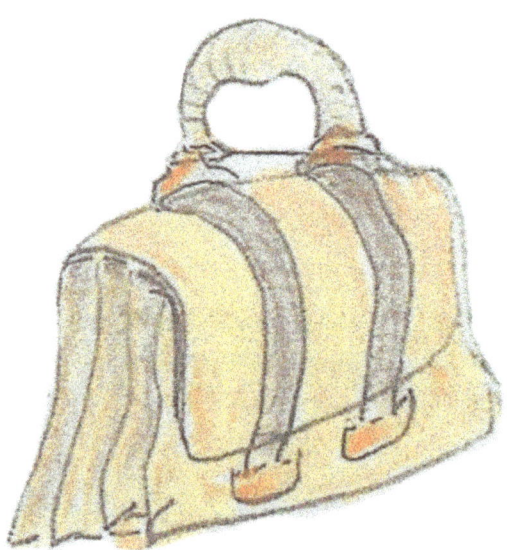

The first (and only) object revealed to the climber, viewed straight ahead through the opening in the ceiling, was a view over powdery dust on the attic floor; there was a weathered, dry leather satchel about thirty inches by twenty-five inches in size, jammed with yellowed papers, many of which were letter-size pages folded into panels 1/3 the length, a sort of artifact used many years ago by banks, courts, and the like. They looked very formal. They did not look like 1948-style "typed" pages from post-World War II.

The author's freehand sketch of the mysterious attic satchel from memory, dating from about 1950. It symbolizes family papers sequestered in an aged leather satchel left on the attic floor at 1706 Farragut in the late 1940s.

After mounting the hatchway into the dust, the boy opened the satchel. In dim light cast up from below, he read documents until it became apparent that some of them were about lunacy and guardianship proceedings in the District Court of Webb County, TX.

A NORSE CLAN CALLED "NYE"

We now intoduce to you two maps from McCrumb's popular text entitled, "The Story of English". The maps are important to the story of Alice Elizabeth Nye's Danish ancestors, who had invaded, and then settled in what is now the main British Island, beginning in about 793 A.D. What the Danes/Norsemen did, over the next 900 years after 793 A.D. was intermarry with Saxon peoples, who you might say, "absorbed" the Norse invaders. The language of British folk in the Eastern counties (of the main British Island) morphed in a period of 900 years into the language of the dissenter migrants who came to Cape Cod shortly after 1620 A.D. When one visits the Nye family reunions held on Cape Cod, to this very day, one is immediately immersed in English pronunciations which came to America (to New England) 389 years ago, with arrival of dissenter-pilgrims, such as Benjamin Nye and his bride Katherine Tupper who came from the Norse or Danish clans. You are about to hear of Benjamin and his family who took part in the initial founding of Sandwich, in Barnstable County, Massachusetts, on Cape Cod.

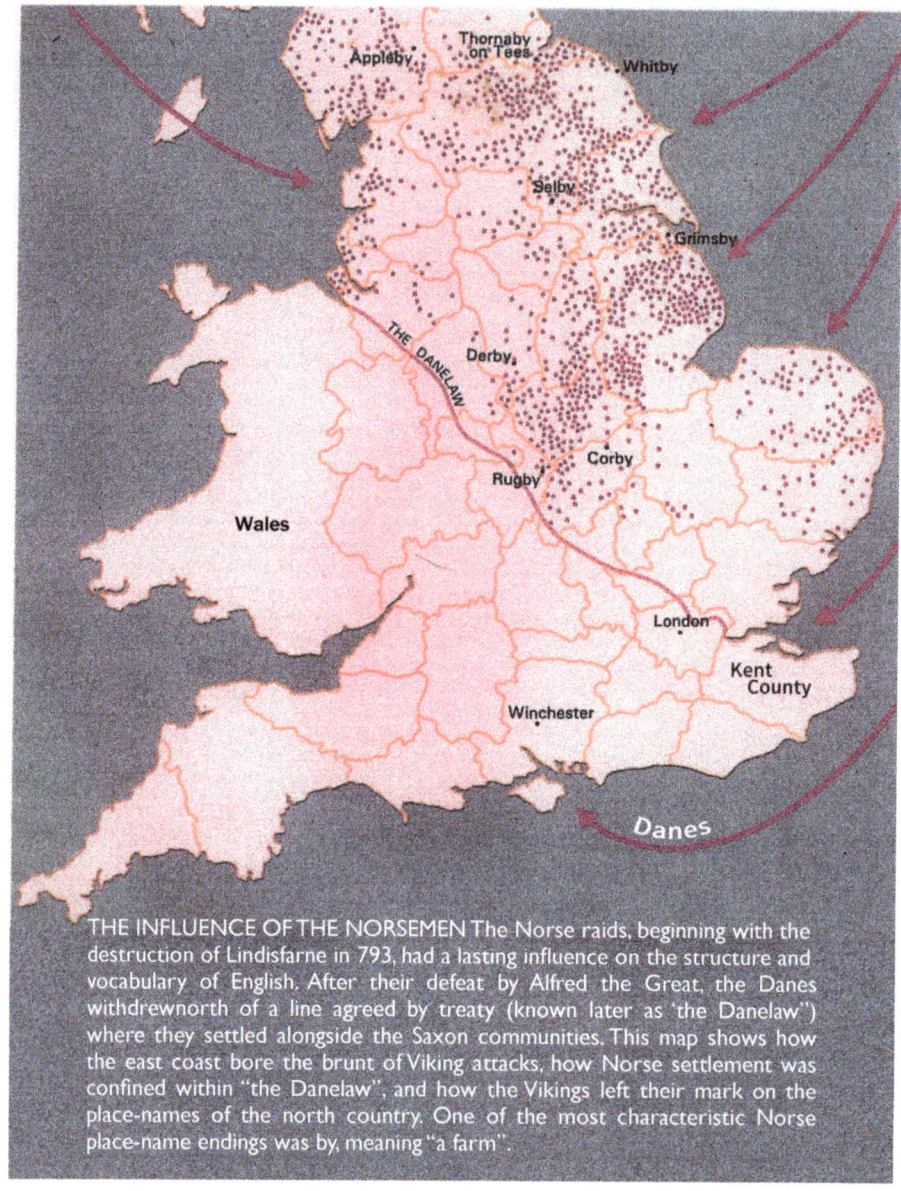

THE INFLUENCE OF THE NORSEMEN The Norse raids, beginning with the destruction of Lindisfarne in 793, had a lasting influence on the structure and vocabulary of English. After their defeat by Alfred the Great, the Danes withdrew north of a line agreed by treaty (known later as 'the Danelaw') where they settled alongside the Saxon communities. This map shows how the east coast bore the brunt of Viking attacks, how Norse settlement was confined within "the Danelaw", and how the Vikings left their mark on the place-names of the north country. One of the most characteristic Norse place-name endings was by, meaning "a farm".

Danish origins

The words "native," "indigenous," and "Indian" are widely used to identify our very own ancestors before we knew who we were as modern, begotten people who came into this world a long time ago.

When Europeans came to Cape Cod (later named Massachusetts), they knew of natives already inhabiting the lands to which they had newly arrived in their flight from European bondage. They knew it was a trade-off.

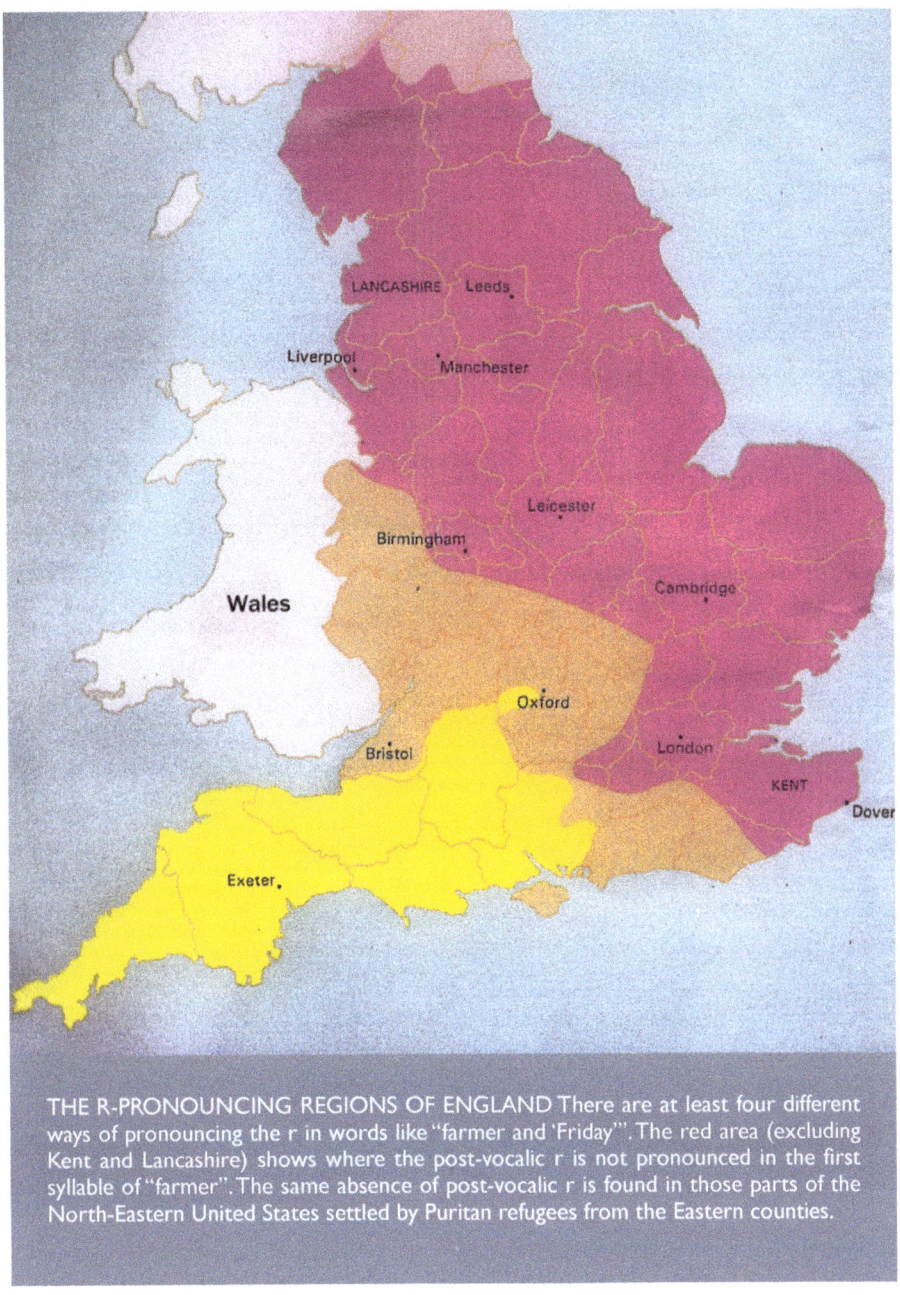

THE R-PRONOUNCING REGIONS OF ENGLAND There are at least four different ways of pronouncing the r in words like "farmer and 'Friday'". The red area (excluding Kent and Lancashire) shows where the post-vocalic r is not pronounced in the first syllable of "farmer". The same absence of post-vocalic r is found in those parts of the North-Eastern United States settled by Puritan refugees from the Eastern counties.

From North America in its "northern" parts, references to native peoples found there gave us tribal names of specific aboriginal clans organized, sometimes loosely, along family relational lines. Indigenous people inhabited the entire North American continent—including what is now Mexico and all of what had been Mexico as far north or west as the *conquistadores* from Spain had traveled. Think of the Norse people and the Danes as virtually "aboriginal" peoples in north Europe! The March 2017 issue of the National Geographic Society Magazine was dedicated to the Vikings. Beautifully the magazine illustrates how many Norse there were and how busy they were before 800 A.D. Thousands of their boats traveled to Greenland, Newfoundland, all of the British Isles, and all over most European waterways, as far east as Russia, even to the doorways to the Middle East and Asia minor.

A daily newspaper cartoon strip, "Hagar the Horrible," makes light (and light-weight) humor of the way of life of the Norse who terrorized all other indigenous peoples, those who had more or less settled down in one place to engage in agriculture, animal husbandry, peaceful trades or crafts. The Norse invaded, pillaged, and killed the locals everywhere they landed their open but ocean-going long boats, propelled by oarsmen. Dig into literature about Norse/Viking raiders, and one plows up the fact that women among Vikings also were warriors! They wielded swords, they would swing them to strike a victim. So, the subject of this biography begins to come into our view as a female warrior. Sometimes a she-bear.

What happened at the monastic island community at Lindisfarne, just offshore in the North Sea from Scotland in the eighth century? Invader-raiders were tough, hardy, and maybe avaricious people whose raids, looting, and pillaging was a "normal" way of life, as we understand the research available. The Norse/Danes did not pack a carry-on bag which fit into an overhead compartment and then head home after a long week in the killing fields. As the years after the obliteration of Lindisfarne rolled into the next century or so, invaders began colonizing various places in the main British island, and then they stayed on and blended in. There was at least "some negotiating" in the second millennium A.D.

The genealogical writers and publishers at The Nye Family Association, Inc., Sandwich, MA, have been at work for about a hundred years, turning out and publishing Nye Family in America data to inform generations of Nyes in the United States who made up their clan in the United States. Volume I of American Nyes of English Origin (Generations 1-8), published in 1977, has a sort of preface entitled "The Nyes in Europe – Denmark." This reports the Nye name began in the thirteenth century in Denmark.

The authors of the prefatory material in Vol. I of the genealogy report, name Nye family heads in Wiltshire, Hampshire, Sussex, Hertford, and Kent, England. The newcomer immigrants to Wiltshire are reported as two brothers, James and Randolf Nye. They had to leave (flee from) a community named "Tudse" in Denmark, because one of them had a duel in the homeland that threatened dire "consequences."

In England, about four generational steps led to the birth of Thomas Nye, whose second wife was Agnes Rye. Their first child, the baby named Benjamin (this being the first English Nye immigrant to New England) was born, on May 4th, 1620. However, the genealogists in Vol. I of the bound genealogy book attributed to this birth a location in County Kent and the village of Biddenden.

Since the publication of Vol. I, an interested genealogist challenged the 1977 attribution of Benjamin's place of birth, and the challenger supported his challenge credibly. As of the September 2017 date on which this author attended a Nye Family in America reunion in Massachusetts, the senior Nye authorities stated to us that the place of Benjamin's entry into the world in 1620 was being researched—again.

However, the Nye family authorities in Sandwich, MA, vouched for the 1977 report that this Benjamin (b. 1620), is one-and-the-same as Benjamin Nye who sailed to Massachusetts on the ship *Abigail* in 1635, during the boy Benjamin's fifteenth year of life. Benjamin appeared as a person of junior status, a subordinate, in the company of ten senior men in Saugus, MA. These ten were in 1637 authorized to go to a location, at what is now Sandwich, MA, to make a new settlement on Cape Cod.

Benjamin had been a protégé of Thomas Tupper, a man thirty years older than Benjamin. Tupper was one of the "ten men of Saugus" who had been assembled to obtain a go-ahead to found the village of Sandwich. Tupper's daughter, Katherine, three years older than Benjamin, was joined in marriage to Benjamin Nye, then age twenty, at Sandwich on October 19, 1640.

And now, for the rest of the story about how, and why, Alice Elizabeth Nye and her paternal granddad T. C. Nye came into our lives at Webb County, Laredo, TX, between the years 1844 through Elizabeth's death in July 2007. The story is a checkerboard with squares of different colors. There are "fits and starts." It is peopled by folks who displayed some noble qualities, which were passed on to generations into the millennium of 2000; it is still being perpetuated in some form, in some poetry, in a lifetime of prose. It is also in people like "the science guy" we see on television.

Pilgrims who sailed on the Abigail in 1635

The first English person in America who was a "Nye" sailed from Plymouth, England, in 1635. He arrived at Boston around October 8th. As we said, he was Benjamin Nye, born in 1620.

The *Geneaology* Vol. 1, page 26, states that by October 1635, 10,000 persons had migrated to the Massachusetts Bay Colony. The Nye genealogy writer said that although Benjamin's father "held a small acreage in Biddenden, long term prospects under an unsettled English government were not good..."

The Story of English states: "... [A]bout two thirds of the early settlers in the Massachusetts Bay area came from the eastern counties...."—i.e., the counties along the eastern coast facing the North Sea, north of London, which by about 1640 had along with East Anglia broken with Charles I and had begun to prepare for war against the king and his established church. Benjamin Nye in his fifteenth year got out of harm's way, ahead of the bloody civil war to come. As a dissenter who did not follow the king, he would have had great difficulty, if not hardship, imprisonment, and death."[2]

What bearing has the history of these dissenters who migrated to Massachusetts Bay Colony upon the life, traits, and personalities of William Newcomb Nye, his immediate children, and grandchildren, including Alice Elizabeth Nye?

The answer is found in the Nyes on Cape Cod, and to the increased rates of adventurousness, generation to later generations. It appears the degree of independence, the extremity of the grit and outspokenness of Nyes who left Cape Cod for *Tejas* (Texas), is history repeating itself. Behaviors after 1835 were being modeled on the action-orientation of Nyes in England, and later, in Massachusetts, after about 1620. But there is more in where it went that Alice Elizabeth Nye comported herself that is modeled, influenced, or even determined by the very makeup of her genes—her genetic inheritance from the English who would not "conform" and Danes or Norse who migrated to England because of events like the outcome of duels.

It is flintiness, my readers, flintiness. Are you beginning to get the picture of the woman who went to Rice in the 1920s and roared poetry and lines of Shakespeare's plays in Room 250 of Martin High? Why, if she had been born male, she may have been Sir John Falstaff reincarnate in her flamboyance.

When we get around to that part of the story, note that the ten men of Saugus who petitioned to go out on Cape Cod to set up a new village were, *ipso facto,* opting out of living in or even near rapidly growing Boston! It was a pattern.

English dissenters: Churchill? Yes!

Regarding the growing unhappiness of the folk who were more Calvinist in their theology than Church of England, they found that their expressions of dissent from the English state church excluded them in many ways from acceptance and protection of their fellow Englishmen and women, and they were actively persecuted in their own home places. None other than Winston Churchill, in his four-volume treatise on *A History of the English-Speaking Peoples,*[3] recognized the facts pertaining to the English people who determined to leave Britain. Churchill wrote, "Many people of independent mind began to consider leaving home (England) to find freedom and justice in the wilds." The rise of the Puritan movement and emigration to New England was described by Churchill as follows:

> "Just as the congregation from Scrooby had emigrated in a body to Holland, so another Puritan group in Dorset, inspired by the Reverend John White, now resolved to move to the New World. After an unhappy start, this venture won support in London and the Eastern Counties among backers interested in trade and aid. After the precedent of Virginia, a chartered company was formed, eventually named "The Company of the Massachusetts Bay in New England." News spread rapidly and there was no lack of colonists. An advance party founded the settlement of Salem, to the north of Plymouth. In 1630 the Governor of the company, John Winthrop, followed with a thousand settlers. He

was the leading personality in the enterprise. The uneasiness of the time is reflected in his letters, which reveal the reasons why his family went. "I am verily persuaded," he wrote about England, 'God will bring some heavy affliction upon this land, and that speedily; but be of good comfort . . . If the Lord seeth it will be good for us, He will provide a shelter and a hiding place for us and others . . . Evil times are coming when the Church must fly into the wilderness."

"Some of the puritan stockholders [i.e. of The Massachusetts Bay Company]realized that there was no obstacle to transferring the company, directors, and all to New England. A general court of the company was held, and this momentous decision taken. From the joint stock company was born the self-governing colony of Massachusetts. The Puritan landed gentry who led the enterprise introduced a representative system, such as they had known in the days before King Charles's Personal Rule. John Winthrop guided the colony through this early phase, and it soon expanded. Between 1629 and 1640 the colonists rose in numbers from three hundred to fourteen thousand. The resources of the company offered favorable prospects to small emigrants. In England, life for farm laborers was often hard. 'Here in the New World there was land for every newcomer. And freedom from all medieval regulations as oppressed and embittered the peasantry at home.'"

VOYAGE TO THE NEW WORLD
◇◇◇◇◇◇◇◇◇◇◇◇◇◇◇◇◇◇◇◇◇◇◇◇◇◇◇◇

In marking the person and character of Alice Elizabeth Nye, it is more than just a little appropriate (her history of ninety-eight years having been made at her life's end in July 2007) to look at her ancestry, the clan from which she was descended. Even in her small place in life, her internal concept of "who she is" was based upon knowing what her family's history consisted of, over several prior generations. As a small child, Captain Thomas C. Nye, grandfather, and Faye McCluskey, her handicapped mother, were focused on grooming her to be formed by a very honed knowledge of the family history, where they had come from and why they got the make-up as persons that were peculiar to just them.

We can recall our own experiences in coming upon a tangible object—let's say a piece of bone, an arrowhead, or a geological specimen lying out in a natural setting in the country. We pick it up in wonderment and turn it over in our hands, viewing it from different angles and in varied light, in some wonderment, and with a resolve to take it with us for further study. This was unique, but at first we did not know what made it so unique or attractive. It took some reflection to go through a changing or evolving mental or emotional process to in effect take in, to breathe in this new, perhaps marvelous thing we had encountered.[4] So, how far back does one go in the process of analyzing a bone fragment found in the wilderness? Naturalists and archaeologists have their methods and reasons, and we who think of cultural and human development over centuries have some additional senses working on this issue. Again, if the nature (genomic heritage) has some peculiarities that invite our concern, we begin to balance the "nurture factors" in development as we proceed. You do not find, very often, on the *Tejas* gulf coast in 1836, or in the warm-climate cultivated onion fields by the Rio Bravo in 1900 clan linkage to (1) Cape Cod on Massachusetts Bay Colony of 1636, or, for another contrast, to (2) dour Calvinist English dissenters from an "establishment" deeply imbedded in British Isles west of the Europe, or, finally, (3) seemingly wild warrior-raiders whose pillaging grounds ranged from a cold, raw, Baltic/North Sea coast into the whole of area between Asia Minor, Greenland, and the rock of Gibraltar at the mouth of the Mediterranean sea.

In order for you to follow our thesis about proclivities of Alice Elizabeth Nye in this biography, you should, at least provisionally, look at the possibility that the "genomes" of Nye generations senior to Benjamin—generations older who came to not only England, but from Scandinavian Europe—had perhaps *the* major effect on formation of the character and the behaviors of Nye persons in each succeeding generation—especially regarding T. C. Nye and granddaughter Alice Elizabeth.

Seven Nye generations following Benjamin in the United States came between 1636 and the eighth generation, which started into birthing (being—*in esse*) about 1878, some of whom lived well into the decade of the 1960s, including, for one example, our great uncle, a son of Thomas C. Nye, namely Chester Wilkinson Nye, b. Dec 9, 1891, at Cotulla, TX. This author, as a son of Alice Elizabeth Nye, can *personally testify* to observing Nye family traits, motives, and actions, because of our positioning, being well-acquainted personally, with Uncle "Chet" and his delightful spouse, Aunt Clara Louise (nee Fletcher), both of whom lived in peppery vigor into their ninth decades.

This author was also acquainted with several other sons of T. C. Nye and several other issue of the children of T. C. Nye (b. May 1844 at Matagorda, TX). We were not ever afforded opportunity to be acquainted with A. P. Nye, Alice Elizabeth's father. Elizabeth never spoke directly to or indirectly about him—her own father—and thereby hangs much of the tale of this biography.

But, from this segue, go back to our main denotation on the Voyage of the *Abigail*, and what came next: The "main man" of this tale is Benjamin Nye. Benjamin was born in County Kent (England) in May of 1620. His mother, Agnes Rye, was the second wife of Thomas Nye. That marriage was sealed ten and a half months before Benjamin's birth. Here are the "facts" arising from *American Nyes of English Origin*, Vol. I, pp. 24-25:

- In his fifteenth year Benjamin joined the company of people on the *Abigail*, a ship said to be ported in London. In 1635 the *Abigail* sailed from Plymouth, England, making landfall ten weeks later at the outer, northern extremity of what is now Cape Cod, MA.

- One account puts the *Abigail's* landing in the New World as Boston, but we confess we are unaware that "Boston" had even been founded as a city with that name before the autumn of 1635.[5] We all have heard many times that the first English ship to land in Cape Cod Bay was, in 1620, the *Mayflower*. Because our topic is Benjamin Nye, we are not relating the stories of immigrants of the *Mayflower* with this company on the *Abigail*, which came about fifteen years later. The point is that Benjamin is the common male ancestor of Alice Elizabeth Nye (b. 1909 at Laredo) and a number of Nyes spread now out over the United State and the world, whose genetic ties emanate from Benjamin and his bride in the year 1640, who was Katherine Tupper, a daughter of Benjamin's mentor, Thomas Tupper. What do genetic "ties" have to do with ancestors alive in 1635, when the topic is a descendant born in 1909 in Texas? It is nature, not nurture at work (i.e., good genes).

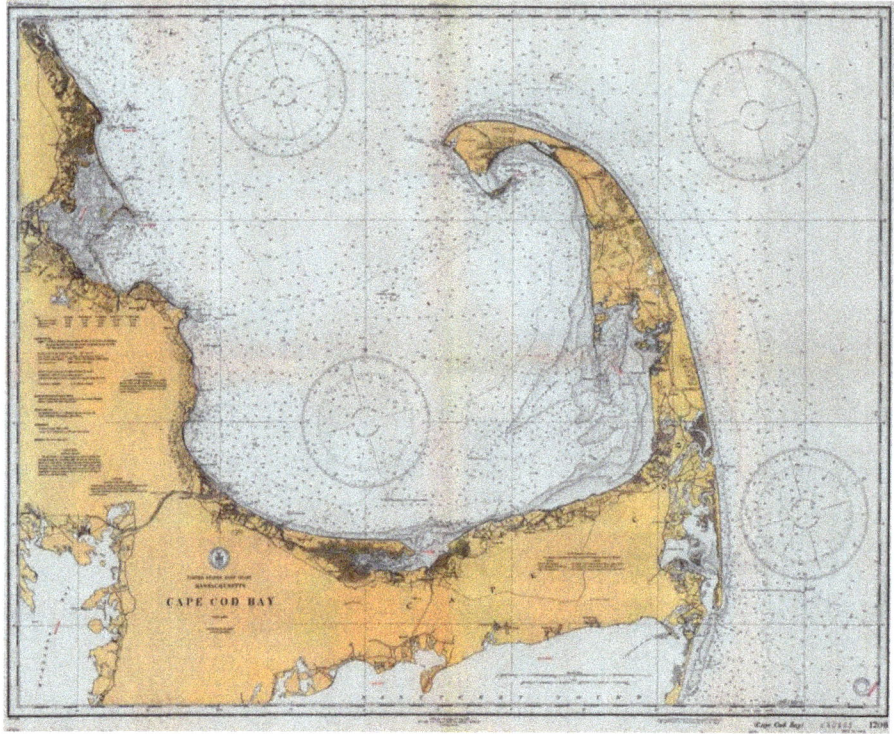

A nautical chart shows us where the *Abigail* went with Benjamin Nye and the Tuppers on board. They might have set foot near where Provincetown is located today. They then went west to the mainland near Saugus. It was from Saugus that they were sent out east on the north shore of Cape Cod to start a village.

What the Nyes experienced at the end of their voyage is described in Appendix 3. To understand the conditions faced by these pilgrims, consider the words of Nathaniel Morton, keeper of the records of Plymouth Colony:

"[T]hey had no friends to welcome them, no inns to entertain or refresh them, no houses, or much less towns, to repair unto to seek for succor; and for the season it was winter, and they that know the winters of the country know them to be sharp and violent, subject to cruel and fierce storms, dangerous to travel to known places, much more to search unknown coasts.

"Besides, what could they see but a hideous and desolate wilderness, full of wilde beasts and wilde men? And what multitudes of them there were, they then knew not; for which way soever they turned their eyes (save upward to Heaven) they could have but little solace or content in respect of any outward object; for summer being ended, all things stand in appearance with a weather-beaten face, and the whole country, full of woods and thickets, represented a wild and savage hew."[6]

Benjamin, a passenger on the *Abigail*, was in the extended family of a man in his 50s, Thomas Tupper. The Tupper group included a girl, Katherine Tupper, age 18. In 1640 Benjamin and Katherine were married in their new house in Sandwich, MA. The records report on several town or community offices discharged by Benjamin and that he was instrumental in establishing mills adjacent to waterways on the edge of Sandwich town.

Why are the details about Benjamin Nye of anything more than passing concern to readers who are not genetically connected to Nye clans in England or Denmark one hundred years before the voyage of the *Abigail*? About one hundred years before the Abigail sailed, two Danish brothers (Bertolf and Randolph Nye) immigrated at various removes to British counties Wiltshire, Hampshire, and/or Sussex, England.

My purpose includes demonstration of how nature more than nurture determined the character of the Nyes of Sandwich, particularly William Newcombe Nye's progeny, Thomas C. Nye and his granddaughter, Alice Elizabeth Nye, nascent in Webb County, Texas, 274 years after Benjamin's settlement on Cape Cod. Notably, Benjamin and family remained in culture "English," despite their association with the cohort of Puritan dissenters, people who are seen as anti-English society and anti-church, even to the point of violence, and even to willingness to give up any loyalty or life blood itself in pursuit of freedom. Let me go further. Please recall similar action by Bertolf and Randolph Nye (of the sixteenth century) and the immigrant to Britain Nyes, rebellious in nature, in spirit (and "in The SPIRIT")—at the seventeenth century then, to stretch the point even more, in strike-out-on-his-own William Newcomb Nye, migrated to Matagorda, *Tejas* (only to drown, ignominiously), then cap it all off by Tom Nye's joinder with the Southern forces and his migration to farming by the Rio Grande at Laredo! Shocking? Improbable? Yes, dizzying.

The Nyes in the century of William Newcomb's departure from Massachusetts

Born in 1764, at Sandwich, MA, Allen Nye was a seafarer, operating a ship named *The William*. When he retired, he went inland to Littleton, MA, where he operated a hotel, but in Sandwich he had fathered eleven children, among them Newcomb Nye, born bout 1805.

It was Newcomb (also called William Newcomb Nye) who moved to the Republic of Texas. The tale of Nyes in Webb County emerges from page 258 of *A Genealogy of American Nyes of English Origin*, Vol. I.

Alice Elizabeth Nye traveled from Laredo to Massachusetts, shortly after her retirement from teaching at Martin High School in 1979, accompanied by her friend, the widow Olive Ray. She bought a hard-bound copy of the published Nye Genealogy Vol. I, during her visit in Sandwich to attend a Nye family reunion. The Texans toured through the Benjamin Nye homestead, near what was Spring Hill, on the pond where Benjamin Nye operated a mill serving the area in what is now Barnstable County, MA.

This bound genealogy book sparked Elizabeth's interest (and mine) in the Nye family. That interest was, shall we say, "fired" by what we are about to remember of that fateful time in 1844 when William Newcomb Nye died in the bay of Matagorda. Left behind were two little boys, William Maynard Nye (b. Nov 1841) and Thomas Carter Nye (b. May 17, 1844).

Page 258 of the "Genealogy" gives these facts: William Newcomb died in January 1844, at which time Eliza Duncan Nye was *enceinte* with the child born in May as Thomas Carter Nye. The mother herself died in May 1844. It was very likely the birthing of Thomas Carter Nye that led to his mother's death "in childbirth" or from complications of the birth.

Our hope is that the current Nye torch-bearers (for lore of the Nye family in America) will regard this work as being of special interest to all Nye descendants everywhere. This is because of peculiar twists and turns in a saga triggered by a Nye who did something unthinkable in the minds of Massachusetts settlers in the new world of almost 200 years ago—by uprooting himself for a wild journey to the southwest part of the continent, necessitating equally wild, survivalist living as his daily lot.

What does the improbable migration of William Newcomb Nye from Sandwich—the comfortable cradle of civilization for four prior generations—have to do with the lives of William's *Tejas* descendants- including Thomas C. Nye, b. 1844 at Matagorda, and his granddaughter, Alice Elizabeth Nye, b. 1909 at Laredo in 1909? The answer is the very reason this author (and others in Texas or Massachusetts and points in between) jumped on a project to amplify, to magnify the life and attainments of Alice Elizabeth Nye, considering enormous adverse, tragic things that were visited upon the characters in our story between 1836 and Elizabeth's death at age 98 in 2007.

More telling is the effect on multitudes of followers, pupils, associates, and readers who have been fascinated by the woman—and her "gospel"— in writing, literature, and ideas she adopted, magnified, and expounded in her productive years, even from childhood through full maturity.

The story of what happened to William and Thomas necessarily involves the intervention of an entire community, led by the members of Christ Church Parish, Matagorda. A later chapter focuses on the Nye family's relationships with the communicants/members of Christ Church Parish on Farragut Street in Laredo, Texas in the first five decades of the twentieth century, and in the latter part of the nineteenth century in LaSalle and Webb Counties (Cotulla and Laredo).

The land promise

If my source for the lore about William Newcomb's travel to *Tejas* in 1835 is correct, this OST overland route used for foot, horse, and wagon traffic by 1835 may have been his route in migration to *Tejas*. From Natchitoches, LA, to Nacogdoches, TX, then Cuero or Goliad, William Newcomb Nye just prior to 1836 had to "bushwhack" his way to the coastal village of Matagorda. Both the written histories of early Tejas and Ms. Julia Hendy of the Nye Family Association suggest that this Nye emigrant did not travel by boat around Florida to New Orleans or Tejas. A settled man from Massachusetts really, really wanted to migrate to do this.

The OST paths demarcated on the map did not lead directly to Matagorda, but ran west- southwest to San Antonio de Bexar and site of the Alamo. A hard left turn off the OST was essential for William Newcomb Nye to approach Matagorda Bay. The early migration mostly followed river courses for travelers to water their horses or mules.

An overland migrant from the East who had come to *Tejas* through Nacogdoches, inside the Louisiana-Texas border, would be entrained down the road to San Antonio. One might then, on reaching the Colorado River's banks, very likely turn southeast, along that bank of the river until he reached the mouth of the river at Matagorda Bay.

Now for the question of why William Newcomb Nye departed from secure Barnstable County and the town of Sandwich, MA, in 1834 or 1835. We also explore the opening of *Tejas* to migrants from the United States, and what that development said to people in Massachusetts. We do not address political or economic conditions in Massachusetts or on Cape Cod that may have contributed to William's motives to "go west," seeking opportunity or wealth—or even a less closely monitored moral and

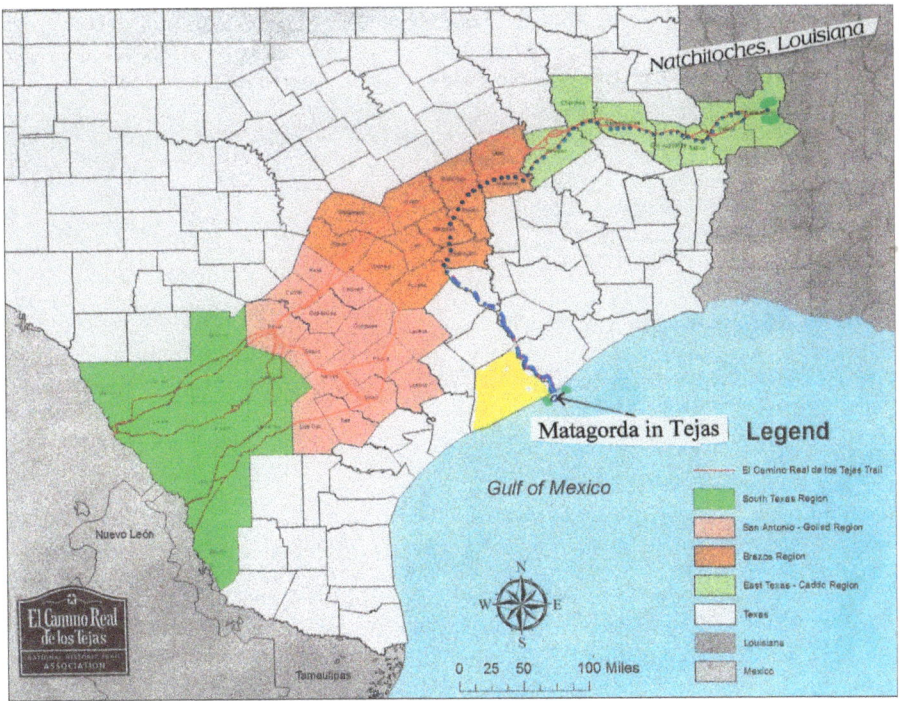

A map of the Old San Antonio Trail (OST) from Natchitoches, LA, into Tejas, to the settlement at Nacogdoches, TX.

personal life. Those motives were large and compelling to many. We leave their exhumation to another time and place and another book, by other authors who echo many other books and research projects covering the two centuries preceding 2019 A.D.

Here, our compass stays fixed on the southwestern trajectories on dry land of one particular third great-grandson of the English emigrant boy, Benjamin, who had first seen light of day in 1620.

What if William Newcomb had thrown his lot in with others who wanted to sail down the east U.S. coast and into the Gulf of Mexico? Such a voyage would have consumed several months, beginning with winter sea conditions on the North Atlantic coast. They would have set out in "nor'easter" winter gales in perhaps January 1835 or 1836. On Matagorda Bay, at the muddy mouth of the Colorado River, the distance sailed would have been nearly 4,000 miles.

Matagorda facts

Principal Routes of Trade and Migration, 1840-1850
Dixon Ryan Fox, *Harper's Atlas of American History* (New York, NY: Harper & Brothers Publishers, 1920)
Downloaded from *Maps ETC*, on the web at http://etc.usf.edu/maps [map #03328]

- T. C. Nye was by community consent (including court action) put into the custody of an elderly English woman, Elizabeth Harvey, who made a home for him—raised him—until he had grown sufficiently to be able to go work in field and farm independently. The work ethic of men on the *Tejas* frontier in the early days of settlement in the Texas Republic was to work to gain a living (or better), which meant long, physical efforts daily to survive.
- Matagorda's Episcopal Christ Church congregation was a large part of T. C. Nye's formation as a child—and his support community—very likely due to his guardian's affiliation with the parish congregation. She may have had affinity for the Church of England while she lived there.
- T. C. Nye became a friend or an employee of Shanghai Pierce, a

local *empresario* who ran cattle in Matagorda County. The relationship was of such standing that T. C. Nye later named one of his sons "Abel Pierce Nye," (b. April 11, 1878). It is easy to surmise T. C. Nye was a protégé' of Mr. Pierce. The lore of early Texas judges Shanghai Pierce to have been a tough, hard-driving man whose family attained wealth.

- T. C. Nye volunteered for service in the Confederate forces who maintained Matagorda's freedom to run supplies through a Union navy blockade of the Texas coast. He was captured and imprisoned by the Union forces.

- At the end of the Civil War in July 1866, T. C. Nye married Frances Elizabeth Shultz, who was of German descent. Years later she died in Laredo, but had insisted that her permanent burial site be in the large Matagorda cemetery. T. C. Nye respected her wishes. Frances Elizabeth Schultz bore T. C. Nye eleven children from 1867 to 1890, one of whom was Abel Pierce Nye (b. 1878, d. 1952). Abel Pierce's marriage to Faye McCluskey produced three children, the eldest one being Elizabeth Nye (b. 1909, at Laredo). Her grandmother Schultz was an immigrant from Europe who had married T. C. Nye in Matagorda.

- The T. C. Nye family migrated west, toward Cotulla in LaSalle County, probably in search of land to put to agricultural uses. At the request of his wife in 1897, the family moved south to Laredo, where a ten-acre farm was created, using irrigation water from the Rio Grande. A local industry for Bermuda onions started with many growers following the Nye farm example with irrigation.

- Frances Nye, having lived in Matagorda, felt Cotulla was lawless, wild, and uncivilized. Matagorda in the period between 1835 and the Civil War in 1861 was one of *Tejas*' better organized areas. Laredo had been settled by Mexican and *mestizo* families who received land grants (on both sides of the Rio Grande) from the viceroy in Saltillo, Coahuila. Laredo was founded in the mid-eighteenth century, before settlements to the north which were peopled by immigrants from the United States. It was regarded as a well-established settlement by 1898.

- Like the motivations driving William Newcomb Nye's migration from Massachusetts to *Tejas* about 1835, the migration of T. C. Nye inland, to the west, was in pursuit of land—an agrarian opportunity. Matagorda and other coastal counties had experienced greater population increase. Perhaps settlement of Matagorda had progressed to a degree that many had arrived and made claims in Matagorda before T. C. Nye was of age to start independent life and due to the 1861 interruption of all lives during the Civil War.

Due to the death of his father in 1844, no land title legacy was secured in William Newcomb Nye's short life. By 1865 other cattle operators had occupied much of the coastal land. So, T. C. Nye felt he had to go west and south from Matagorda. Books and films about the early Southwest have focused on competition between cattle operators and farmers for land.

William N. Nye's migration happened 200 years after his ancestors (Benjamin Nye included) had arrived in the Plymouth Colony. It is generally accepted that people came to the Texas Republic betting on the United States expansion into Texas after about 1830.

The motive must have been similar to the motives of all the others on the eastern seaboard: A promise of land from an organizer of colonies. Still, one may wonder why would they leave a safe, established life in New England for the wilds of *Tejas*? In Sandwich, MA, the Nyes had fresh water, neighbors, and trees and operated a sawmill. It is clear that the promise of an award of land piqued the curiosity of the men who considered a Texas journey. Publicity about Mexico's approval of Stephen F. Austin's colony only fed the incentive for William N. Nye to plan his journey to Texas. When one considers the history from 1630 to 1836, an examination of the minds and the actions of the settlers from the northeastern settlements leads only to land as the motivation.

Matagorda: Marriage of W. N. Nye and Elizabeth Duncan

William Newcomb Nye and his bride, Ms. Elizabeth Duncan, in Matagorda, TX, in 1837.

It is striking to recall that seven years after these photographs, not only had William Newcomb Nye gone down with his boat in a storm, probably not far from his land grant home, but also that almost immediately his wife, pregnant with the baby Thomas C. Nye, died so soon after the birth. It leaves one breathless to contemplate the tragedy of this little family so recently following William Newcomb's arrival and land grant. Our research is not complete on William Newcomb Nye. He appears in the *American Nyes of English Origin* and within the family canon. Elizabeth requested research from a genealogist in Matagorda County. Here is the man, recently off the Camino Real starting in Natchitoches, LA, newly married, and the Gulf storms take him. Then his wife, perhaps suffering preeclampsia—and there are on the raw frontier two boys, with nothing left but the surrounding community of a few hundred hard-up people of Matagorda. But in that few hundred a church had just been founded.

The link between William Newcomb Nye's boys and the solid, established life of Sandwich, MA, was eradicated. How was continuity between the little boys and their Dad's roots on Cape Cod, MA, ever to be regained? It fell to Elizabeth to start research of the connection.

The next iteration of the story of Elizabeth Nye's links to Massachusetts blood lines is perforce the surviving orphan, Thomas C. Nye, nurtured in the bosom of a church community started only a few years before William Newcomb Nye arrived in *Tejas*.

GENETICS AS DESTINY
◇◇◇◇◇◇◇◇◇◇◇◇◇◇◇◇◇◇◇

A "genome" is defined as
"one complete haploid set of chromosomes."

The genetic inheritances of William Newcomb Nye (and his spouse, Ms. Duncan) figure very prominently in what has been said, and what will be said, about Alice Elizabeth Nye's genetics, which "amplified" who she was in terms of character traits that were displayed to the communities she inhabited until 2007.

Dying in 1844, what William Newcomb Nye "had in him" was immediately preserved in Thomas Carter Nye, in his very body, In this hour, the infant was protected by being made by court order a ward of his English nanny, Elizabeth Harvey. The two little Nye boys carried in their genome the building blocks of their family clan ancestry. Nye clan was ingrained in them, engrafted in their very essence, in the very marrow of their bones. They were "programmed" like fine, wool-bearing sheep from a county fairground. No science guy did it; it was managed by the BIG force, known from the Book of Genesis.

What are the implications of this start for all of us who knew Alice Elizabeth Nye as the "net product" of William Newcomb and Thomas C., even Abel Pierce Nye?

You readers must write down the names, dates of birth, and deaths of each of your own maternal and paternal ancestors as far back as you can go beyond your immediate parents. Inscribe them in a scroll secured in a Hebraic phylactery, to be worn on a leather band tied on to your forehead, thereby adorning your very soul. What you will have done is to "put on" the attributes of your very body, blood, tissue of your brain and soul, from your toenails to the tip end of each hair on your head. If you want to "see" yourself as God created you as an individual, then do this. He created you with genes. This is one way to know, to fully appropriate who you are.

This story of Alice Elizabeth replicates, for her, when she was here, the "who she was." What we became suffused with, and that which we absorbed, drank in as her very essence, mirrored you—all those she encountered—and reflected back to all of us who were with her, in Classroom 250, and outside it, beyond it, even into this present day.

What we preach here is that her nature was to be with and in you, reflecting you and your essence to all the world around you, to your family, to all your brothers and sisters of your clan and tribe, whether in her voice and poetry—which you heard in her presence—or in the lines she wrote about you in the *Laredo Times,* the *South Texas Citizen,* and *La Re Dos,* with a little *San Antonio Express News* thrown in for good measure. This is how she lived in love for you! Her genes were loving you.

This chapter began with meditation on William N. and wife, Elizabeth Duncan, in the *Tejas* land rush in the Stephen F. Austin colony. By May 1844 they were wiped out, merest chaff left after God's harvest. Among the chaff were remnants, left living flesh and blood—two children in very dire straits, two progenies, vulnerable like "fingerlings," minnows in a mossy pond occupied by hungry big fish.

How can I put it to you about genes of Alice Elizabeth Nye, in order to drive home the arrows that are the genes, her links to Massachusetts Nye blood lines? Genes transmitted from 1636 (and earlier) determined in very large measure the warp and weft of Alice Elizabeth Nye's physical traits, personality, mental health, and cognitive ability—and her longevity. I invite you to consider "Our Fortune telling Genes," an article by Dr. Robert Plomin published November 16, 2018, in *The Wall Street* Journal, which begins:

"A new tool for analysis of hundreds of thousands of small genetic differences can predict a range of psychological attributes from birth (of an individual). It will transform how we see ourselves, our capacities and our problems. . . .

"About 99% of the six billion steps in the spiral staircase of DNA's double helix are the same for us all. This is what makes us human. Behavioral geneticists are interested in the 1% of the DNA that makes us *individuals*. . . . What may come as a surprise is that DNA also accounts, on average for 50% of the differences between individual persons in psychological traits such as personality, mental health, cognitive ability and disability, *as well as ability and aptitude*."

We report to you that the Nyes of Denmark, Norway, and the Danelaw for the last 900 years (or more) poured their collective program into the body of Alice Elizabeth. It is what *made* Alice Elizabeth Nye! Environment could not pull down the "temple" of this lady. Environment was almost nothing in the light of her genome, especially that flintiness! Perhaps this is true for some of us as well.

As for T. C. Nye: A mere boy exerted himself naturally to be in cattle raising on the Texas Gulf Coast during the time of the Republic of Texas. It went with T. C.'s work as a cowman for Shanghai Pierce. Pierce was a man of some fame in the days of the open land before barbed wire separated land on which a given entrepreneur could count on confining, and therefore managing, a herd to call his own.

Note, when you read of Nye men and families who emigrated to Massachusetts, the foundling, T. C. Nye had no prospect of going off to a

New England college or seminary, and regardless of the cultural heritage of his ancestors back in Cape Cod, they knew not of an intellectual world that had fostered immigration of their ancestors from England to the shores of Cape Cod in 1635. Religious dissent of Massachusetts Bay Colony founders from the "established" Church of England got to be a less-than-conscious factor for our Nyes in *Tejas*. Mere survival was a priority, a necessity, as it had been in 1635.

Newborn foundling, Thomas, was my great-grandfather. In my childhood I learned a great deal about him from my mother, Elizabeth. Her grandpa was a living, breathing, and vital presence at 1706 Farragut Street. When that house was demolished in 1962, I cried in the vision of his ghost cemented under the floor of a warehouse!

Their journeys over the years were marked by connectedness to faith communities where there was mutual love and respect of many families of both Protestant and Roman Catholic persuasions.

THE ORPHAN AND PROTECTED PERSON

A foundling in 1844, T. C. Nye was nurtured by Elizabeth Harvey, a member of Christ Church Episcopal Parish at Matagorda, TX, and a surrogate parent.

On the main floor of Penrose Hospital Main in Colorado Springs hangs a large oil painting of three nuns of a Roman Catholic order sitting in front of a convent door, one of whom has an infant swaddled in her lap, implying that the infant was left at the convent as a foundling. Such were the frequent scenes in history in Western Europe. This orphaning of Thomas Carter Nye (b. 17 May 1844) in Matagorda, TX, upon his mother's death in May 1844 was a theme repeated here. Picture a newborn baby all alone.

We have little to say in this book about elder brother William Maynard Nye, other than he died in June 1890, and little else is known.

We assume the orphaning of T. C. Nye was the result of complications of the baby's birth. Think of images of destitute children as orphans throughout history in the West from war, pestilence, short life-spans, and lack of institutions for care. Churches organized in the New World readily adapted to good works for orphan babies as a broader extension of "established" churches in Europe before 1620.

The community took steps for formal appointment of a guardian for the child, Thomas. Mrs. Harvey was a member of the parish because as her immigration from Britain implies, she was familiar with the English state church and its U.S. affiliates. We have not yet researched the facts of Mrs. Harvey's family and birth in England. Christ Church Parish in 1844 was organized as a Christian community in the Republic of Texas given demographics and society's organization (or disorganization) in Matagorda in the Austin Colony of the Texas Republic. We suggest the bare facts of abject need of little Thomas in his first few days in May 1844 indicates that his nanny and guardian would have presented infant, Thomas, to Christ Church for baptism and that the church members and leadership saw to it that provision was made by the community for the upbringing of the child.

Christ Church was founded in 1844 and was the first Anglican church in Texas. (Photo courtesy of Christ Church parish in 2015.)

In 1844 in *Tejas*, Nye family-of-the-blood could step up to adopt a foundling baby. That was not so practical for Nye family members thousands of miles away from the Texas Gulf Coast. Comparing our readers' world of material wealth (and your circumstances) with conditions on frontiers in Western North America, we need not go far to paint the dire picture of life in early *Tejas* before the dawn of its acceptance as a part of the United States.

Shanghai Pierce commemorative statue in Blessing, TX.

Regardless of cultural backgrounds and whether we as Nye descendants are of Protestant heritage or believers in the Mother Church, normal practice from the seventeenth to twenty-first centuries has been to cherish Christian baptism of all newborn children.

We realize New World systems that hold infant baptism as inappropriate—the notion that persons must be near adulthood to grapple with, know, and accept the Christian life (or be formally subjected to catechism before participation in sacramental life)—are still in vogue. But the simple folk on the Texas frontier practiced infant baptism as handed down to them by their Catholic, Anglican, or Lutheran fathers. Of course, many had no religion at all.

However, raw survival on the frontier put steel in the people, encouraging fellowship, acceptance of Christ, and the comfort enjoyed by Christian people of God. Sacraments flowed in with the people.

Newspapers and correspondence report that Thomas C. Nye went into service of the Confederate States of America at Matagorda, and he engaged in patrol of the Gulf Coast to counter blockading vessels of the Union. Anecdotes from Elizabeth speak of her grandfather's service experience as including not one, but two, captures by Union forces and imprisonment. Research does not disclose whether he was released in an exchange of prisoners or, possibly, escaped from captivity. There was no report of his being wounded or disabled.

As a child and young adult in a community with oversight of his nanny between 1844 and the outset of the Civil War in 1861, Thomas must have had knowledge of his own father's (William Nye) origin in Massachusetts.

He may have been in direct contact with Nye relatives in Massachusetts after the war. Being a resident of *Tejas*, between the year it was made a part of the Union by treaty (about 1845) and the outbreak of the Civil War, it is not surprising that T. C. Nye threw in his lot with friends in Matagorda; Texas was part of the slave-holding states, tied to the economy of the South, from the inception of *Tejas* settlement. As far as T. C. Nye knew, Matagorda was the only home-place he enjoyed as an orphan whose immediate family had been wiped out in 1844.

What is known and documented about the courtship and arranged marriage of Capt. Nye's son, Chester (b. Dec. 9, 1891, Cotulla, TX,), with Clara Louise Fletcher, at Littleton, MA, suggests Chester went to New England for the purpose of courtship after his tenure of a few years as a student of Texas A & M College. Capt. T. C. Nye and the Fletcher family in Massachusetts were very likely introduced by long-time Nye family residents in Littleton, MA.

Genealogy records document that Allen Nye (b. August 5, 1764, at Sandwich, MA.), Chester Wilkinson Nye's great-grandfather, was survived by descendants who were still in or near Littleton, MA, eighty years or so after Allen's death there on July 20, 1825. We infer that Nyes in Littleton or thereabouts were instrumental in communication with T. C. Nye after 1865, and maybe before Chester's birth in Cotulla in 1891. Loyalties owed by T. C. Nye to Nyes in Massachusetts appear to have been rekindled after he survived the Civil War, regardless of whether the Matagorda ancestor had taken arms for the defeated Confederacy.

Typical cattle drive crew. (Photo courtesy Library of Congress.)

On the other hand, T. C. Nye's affiliation with the Southern side may have been an expression of natural loyalty that the orphaned Nye boy may have felt to his Matagorda community in 1861. There may have been a conflicting, but much more remote loyalty for the distant North. Perhaps it would not have been too unusual for there to arise rekindled affection between Nyes in the North and their cousins in the South—years after Civil War hostilities ended.

By assorted correspondence fragments and references in newspapers, we learn T. C. Nye and family stayed at least for a few months in Cotulla, TX, in a migration that ultimately ended in Webb County, at Laredo, near 1897 or 1898. The time-line sequence marking Nye migration after the Civil War:

- T. C. Nye and Frances Elizabeth Shultz married at Christ Church, Matagorda, July 12, 1866.

- In 1870 Elizabeth Harvey, the guardian who reared Thomas C. Nye in his orphaned childhood, resided with him and Frances at Matagorda. Elizabeth Harvey, apparently a member of Christ Church community, was an immigrant probably from Britain, but one source believed she was from Russia.

- Between the end of the Civil War and the 1870 census, Grandpa Nye was probably serving in cattle-culture. A newspaper article after the family moved to the farm at Laredo contains details about Grandpa Nye's affairs in Cotulla, as if he had not merely sojourned to look at farming prospects there for a few months, but the family may have settled in LaSalle County for a few years.

- We were given an anecdote by Elizabeth as to why the Nyes moved south of Cotulla near the end of the eighteenth century. It seemed Grandmother Nye (Frances Shultz Nye) had seen, from a house window, the lynching of a man. The experience caused Ms. Nye to ask Grandpa Nye that the family plan to move out of Cotulla to a more "civilized" locale, which might render for the family a sense of order and decorum.

- The migrations of T. C. Nye and family can in part be traced by analysis of the births, adult life attainments, or deaths of T. C. Nye's offspring. Our initial review was simply to see who had survived to adulthood and to note whether they were born in Matagorda county, or later, perhaps in Cotulla.

Here is an enumeration of children born to T. C. Nye and Frances Shultz Nye from 1867-1900:

- A son, Walter, b. 1867—died 1874.

- A son, Thomas, b.1869—survived one day.

- These two babies were born, died, and were buried in Matagorda. We have checked the numerous Nye family graves to gain added insight.

- A son, Frank William, b.1871—survived to adulthood, married to Ollie Callum in 1892. (Three of his children were born from 1892 through about 1898.)

- A daughter, Annie Elizabeth, b. July, 1873-married Dr. W. E. Johnson, died at about age 27, survived by one child aged about six years old.

- One researcher listed in the Nye genealogy at p.440 a child, Henry, b.1875—died Jan., 1881 (age nine). (The local research by Elizabeth in Matagorda County did not list such a boy in the eighth generation, and we are not sure about that matter.) Additional records search is necessary, but Henry is recorded as having died at age six.

- A son, Abel Pierce, b. April 11, 1878—died February 7, 1952. He attained adulthood, but his life was more than a bit difficult, as we shall see later. He fathered three children—one of whom is the heroine in this book, Alice Elizabeth.

- A daughter, Florence Elizabeth, b. Aug 27, 1880—died April 11, 1882 (aged one year and a few months).

- A daughter, Fannie, b. 1882—lived to adulthood, married to Allan B. Collins.

- A son, Grover Cleveland, b. 1885—lived to adulthood and farmed at Dilley, Texas.

- A daughter, Ethel Carlan, b. 1889—died after one week.

- A son, Chester Wilkinson, b. 12-9-1890, at Cotulla, Texas—lived to be an adult, well into his nineties, was a student at Texas A & M University, and married Clara Fletcher at Littleton, MA., in 1912.

The circumstances suggest that the Nyes, lately of Matagorda as of 1870, did not depart Cotulla for Laredo until after the birth of Chester Wilkinson Nye, the Nye descendant who later visited Littleton, MA, and married Clara Louise Fletcher, daughter of Elmer Warren and Minnie Hartwell Fletcher.

FAMILY FERMENT

Our introduction to the family ferment starts with this letter, written in 1906 to Faye McCluskey, then a resident of Galveston, Texas:

A letter from A. P. Nye to Faye McCluskey while they were courting in 1906. There is more to A. P. Nye than the profound character faults—things suggesting once upon a time, before he became mentally ill or hopelessly addicted, he had decency, and may have been a "good soul". His humanity as of 1906 is demonstrated by a yellowed, original letter he wrote to his fiancee, Faye, which is pictured here, but we have taken a magnifying glass to it, and translated his rough script with additional comments by us, and it is found in the Appendices, page 107, following the newspaper obituary for Alice Elizabeth which precedes it.

What I set forth in this chapter was discovered as a result of my investigation, or by happenstance digging, into the attic of the ancestral house at 1706 Farragut Street. The first attic adventure occurred in about 1949 or 1950. I was in late childhood pre-puberty. The attic foray began because, by 1950, there was an atmosphere of mystery, my feeling of goings-on not discussed by anyone in the family, picked-up by "default" of a telling of truth by virtually everyone with whom this boy was associated—everywhere. We are dealing here with what was *not-said*, more than what was actually aired or spoken-of. The only son of Mrs. Alice Elizabeth Nye Sorrell noticed that he had *never had any conversation* with his mother about her own father, Abel Pierce Nye. The impression fostered was that he had 'died a long time ago'. The next two photos are to introduce images of the Nye family at times when he had been present for these next two photos, prior to World War I. On the farm, or at grandpa Nye's house these family group pictures show there was a whole cast of characters—and most of the cast had melted-away before Alice Elizabeth had either entered Old High School, or the year she began her Rice Institute studies in Houston, Texas. Where did they all go and were all of them dead or moved-away?

Nye family group at Christmas 1915 posed against the yellow-brick wall outside Grandpa Nye/s house in town.

Prior to 1929, tragedy upon tragedy had overcome the people in the photos shown above. Between 1914 and 1920 arthritic/joint-destroying disease of Elizabeth's mother had confined her first to a wheelchair, a paraplegic. In the years we researched the history for this biography, we have begun to wonder if her illness and taking to her bed was accompanied by emotional wounds caused by "loss" of husband A. P. Nye. Or was financial ruin and loss of the farm also at work.

People in the photo at the Nye family farm in North Laredo, Webb County, TX, near the north bank of the Rio Grande River. From left, Frank William Nye; wife Allie Callum; Faye McCluskey, wife of A. P. Nye, holding infant Charlene Frances Nye (b. Jan. 25, 1911); Frances Elizabeth Shultz, wife of Capt. Thomas Carter Nye (bearded man with galluses, then about age 67). The toddler in the foreground is Alice Elizabeth, sister of Charlene. Miles Nye has not been born yet. Frank William Nye holds an onion in his right hand.

Abel Pierce Nye, Elizabeth's father, had developed alcohol addiction and a wildness for "bad women" who lived near the railroad depot. He is reputed to have stayed at the Hamilton Hotel with friends of bad repute, scandalizing the Nye family and friends. He was adjudicated a lunatic by a Webb County judge, and the family endured foreclosure on the Nye farm around the beginning of World War I.

Yet, during the period before 1924, Faye McCluskey Nye insisted on continued piano lessons for pre-teen Elizabeth. The family groomed her for "better things," including post-high school education at Rice. How did that happen? Nyes who lived at the Farragut Street house of Thomas C. Nye, in 1920 included Faye, now an "invalid," plus Elizabeth Nye, Miles C. Nye, and their sister Charlene Frances. Grandpa Nye died in 1917, but no one has mentioned the flu epidemic during that era. Below is the so-called Victorian style house, located at 1706 Farragut Street, Laredo, TX., It was two blocks west of the main business district and the square called Jarvis Plaza.

Pictured are Miles C. Nye and his wife shortly before the end of World War II. Miles and Alice Wade Nye are leaning against the cast iron picket fence, facing the camera aimed from the south, across Farragut St. He had been in the Army Air Corps and she had served as an Army nurse in battle in Europe.

U. S. Census for 1930 identifies Elizabeth, her younger siblings, Miles and Charlene, as residents with their aunt, Inez McCluskey Shipplett, in Houston during the year 1931 in which Elizabeth completed her B.A. degree at Rice Institute, now Rice University. Also resident there was Mrs. Shipplett's father, Charles McCluskey, by then in his seventies, a widower.

Just prior to 1930, Elizabeth's mother, Faye, had died in Laredo, where she was buried. The Farragut Street home was rented, due to the departure of all the family. The south Texas scion of the Nyes who were descended from William Newcomb Nye, the pioneer, our beloved Grampa—Thomas Carter Nye—died in August, 1917, in Laredo, where he is buried. "Auntie" Inez nee McCluskey became surrogate parent to A. P. Nye's children after 1917 to set the scene in Houston, Harris County, Texas, where Alice Elizabeth's coming to maturity at Rice Institute took full flower.

Old High School. Because Old High school's location on the Plaza where the town had been founded, so we direct your eye to a photo of the Plaza fronting Old High on its South Side, and fronting St. Augustine Cathedral on the East of the Plaza. This was the scene for Old High. It must have been crossed by Alice Elizabeth to walk to Farragut Street to the North and West of this landmark.

Picture Alice Elizabeth in her late teens and approaching age twenty, working at hospital telephone switchboard for long hours, doing her Rice class reading at night, at work, then, getting on the Main Street trolley, then to dismount at Rice Boulevard, to walk, day or night-time, frequently in Rain at least a mile from there to her aunt Inez's house. In a place and time when college folk did not have automobiles, she studied successfully and earned income for her upkeep at the Shipplett home. She had a fine worthy work ethic.

St. Augustine Plaza, the founding point for the city.

I beg you to recall, for a moment the young girl child (in a Prince Valiant hairstyle, a bob) who had been groomed for a formal education by Capt. Thomas C. Nye and Elizabeth's invalid, nearly paraplegic, mother. Refer back to the Prologue, where her childhood photo in that Prince Valiant style for a sharpened sense about her at that time, when she was only 10 or 12. The nurturing of that child in music, literature, and arts—all The Humanities—was carried on during years of family travails before, during and until a little after World War I.

But, dear Nye family and others of the Webb County community here is the hard part: A Court lunacy proceeding for Abel Pierce Nye covered several months, leading to his hospitalization in a Texas State asylum in San Antonio. The grim image of the father's crushing, public humiliation must be superimposed over the light, cheerful visions we portray here of the nurture of the girl up until her mother's death. We ask the reader to visualize young Alice Elizabeth Nye in the high school, within easy walking distance of the T. C. Nye homestead, at 1706 Farragut Street, several blocks west of the plaza where St. Augustine Church towered over the square, facing west. Carry that image, if you will, along into this next image: Being eldest of three siblings, Alice Elizabeth became "head" of the remaining Nye family, presided over by her handicapped mother and her widower grandfather. She was the only mentally, emotionally, and physically equipped person in the Laredo Nye family household from age eight (in 1917), through the year 1927, which was on the threshold of her move to Houston to live with aunt, Inez Shipplett, near the Rice campus. Many of you will recall families in which, due to enforced absence, death, or disability of one or both parents, the eldest female child became the strength, the motivator for younger siblings still needing supervision, and the duty falls to this one as home health caregiver to aged and sick adults in the household. Instead of squalor we see, acted-out, a story of strength and redemption, not unlike stories Alice Elizabeth heard on Sundays, inside Christ Church Parish (Episcopal) the door of which was only 300 feet outside the wrought iron front gate at 1706 Farragut Street.

As I "project" reminiscences of my own childhood in Laredo, it is indelible in my mind, as it must have been in my mother's soul: Savor, contemplate, touch with my hand, the front facade of old high school, faced north on the plaza, the back elevation facing Mexico, south, only a few hundred yards distant, looking down upon the north bank of the Rio Grande. The historicity of the square, its monuments, and the neighboring buildings sited at the founding of the town of Laredo (about 1747) requires some embellishment of Elizabeth's story, because of the setting on the San Augustin plaza. Next to the High School structure, abutting it on the east, is a low, single-story structure which had been the capital of a government of The Republic of The Rio Grande which had endured in some form from 1840 to 1842. Instead of Christmas eves past, I am reminded of ghosts like old Marley in Dicken's tale, A Christmas Carol, when I breath-in the footpads of souls long gone who traversed these streets and Plazas in blazing sunny weather year-round.

Again, to draw on lore at our command, we see also during her high school tenure, in 1927, Alice Elizabeth was hired by the Laredo Times newspaper to be a "cub" reporter, due in part to her journalism work at Old High. Odilon Arambula's "A Laredo Legend" . . . published in the Laredo Morning Times, to commemorate Elizabeth's 97th birthday in January 2006, said:

> "Researching material by Times writers . . . Jim Falvella and Star Castillo, we rediscovered Mrs. Sorrell in her roles, first as a reporter and assistant editor of the school paper, and then editor in her senior year (1927) . . . we first heard stories at Martin High School . . . of her strange accounts of tiger football games, getting (paid) ten cents a (column) inch, which caught the attention of the Times editor, William Prescott Allen.

"... She called for a change in colors of the Tiger football team uniforms. It became the subject of a school student assembly ... Thereafter, the newspaper published another article by Miss Nye ... on the need to expand and improve school curriculum, listing courses in the language arts (writing and journalism), sciences and social studies, economics, business, vocational training, physical education, a library, etc. ... The principal took notice. The superintendent took notice. The school board took notice and heard from the advocates with what the young woman detailed in the essay. It planted the seeds that meant ... within the next decade, Laredo would have a brand-new state of the art high school—Raymond and Tirza High School. That summer of 1927 the Times editor, Mr. Allen, hired her as a reporter at $10 per week ... and, within the decade, Laredo had voted bonds to match the federal funding for the new school."

This author visited Odilon Arambula on Saturday, December 1, 2016, at offices of the Laredo Morning Times in Laredo for the purpose of soliciting Odi's support and hands-on cooperation in the preparation of this biography. Bill Green was there. We offered to him the AUTHORSHIP and direction of this very Publication!

We did not know at the time that Odilon, in 2016, was under treatment for cancer. He died early in 2018, having been too ill to become involved in our research or writing. It explained his lack of response to our request that he undertake authorship or editing of this our manuscript. It still is a great loss to experience his passing. With loss of my classmate, Mr. Arambula, as an advocate for this work, our access to resources in records of the Laredo Morning Times and others in the Laredo community has been circumscribed. Few people in Texas knew and worked with Mrs. Elizabeth Nye Sorrell as closely, and loyally, as Odilon from 1951 to the end of her life in July, 2007.

What is clear from the foregoing material is that Alice Elizabeth Nye, at age fifteen, sixteen, and seventeen, already had begun a singular career of advocacy for her pupils, the administration, and staff in the schools and in her contribution at age eighteen as a working journalist in Laredo. She immersed herself in its public life and the lives of her many pupils who later became fellow journalist- advocates (such as Odilon Arambula decades later) with a high level of energy and zeal, sufficient to transcend any burdens on her daily and nightly effort in family care-giving at home to her mother and her two younger siblings, Miles Nye and Charlene F. Sinclair (nee Nye).

Now we take a temporary leave of Mrs. Sorrell's years prior to 1928. Rice Institute! Time-travel with us to Houston:, Rice Institute, founded by William Marsh Rice, between the era of the Peace of Paris, in 1919, Woodrow Wilson's time into the "roaring" twenties and early thirties. This was when Elizabeth grew from Rice scholar, working her way through school on a shoestring, to her 1934 courtship by Norman W. A. Sorrell, in Laredo in the mid 1930s.

To review, see from a bird's eye view, your trip with me from the mid to late nineteenth century. See the NYE onion farming years, then hardship years for the Nye family, which befell them before the economic Depression, the pre-World War II era. Why reflect on my parent now? I am compelled to reflect, because I am flesh-and-blood progeny of our heroine. But, dears, this story is really about *you*, if you are a south-Texan, an advocate for our border people, if you are female; or if you carry a flag for education or human rights in a loving community! What I say here is not about me, nor about what's left of Nye family descendants in Texas, so much as it is about you—it is we—the United States of America, daily pulsating with international trade as the linch-pin in our southern borders to the larger world itself. Onion farming years of the Nyes through World Wars I and II and Elizabeth's childhood in Laredo, comfortably housed at 1706 Farragut Street were, were, in fact, "dark". Those years were not felt in shame by Alice Elizabeth. The human spirit of Alice Elizabeth Nye thrived in the austerity and difficulty of her family.

So much had happened to the Nyes, it stoked the fire of Elizabeth's character, but if or when, I tell you "why and how," it will be more even remarkable to see it—viewed through lenses mounted on our noses from 1950 or later.

MEN OF GERMAN DESCENT
◇◇◇◇◇◇◇◇◇◇◇◇◇◇◇◇◇◇◇◇◇◇◇◇◇

While in her senior year at Rice she encountered the attentions of one man. He was Elizabeth's German language professor at Rice University, Heinrich Meyer. We are bemused, this writer, thinking of Alice Elizabeth, the girl who lived with her Aunt Inez Shipplett on Rice Boulevard, operating a hospital telephone switchboard after hours to support her school program, a girl who walked three miles a day/night on a muddy path between Auntie's house and the Main Street trolley to work and school—that she was the object of the lecherous eye of middle-aged Professor Heinrich Meyer.

The wide-eyed girl was treated to dinner at the Rice Hotel Roof nightclub. There are in our archive several letters from him to Elizabeth suggesting she go with him to Germany, where he expected to enjoy the fruits of the new order, the Third Reich, founded by Adolph Hitler and the Nazi party. The letters are the most salacious single piece of archival content left to us by Elizabeth, although in this day and time it is difficult to imagine how a University-educated German male could possibly be romantically and foolishly inclined to put his thoughts in writing to a nubile young student at Rice Institute nearly twenty years his junior! Elizabeth naively engaged the teacher in the college in wonderment of what Europe was like, or how was it to be German at that time, much as she did frequently engage English Literature Professor George Williams of the Rice faculty over four years of her undergraduate career.

Elizabeth kept in touch with Prof. Williams (no, not Prof. Meyer) over many years after her Rice career, and I recall her account of several literary-topic conversations she had with Prof. Williams, both during and after her Rice attendance. Obviously, from the altruism Elizabeth acted out virtually as a lifestyle in her Laredo teaching and, later, in her two-year Master of Arts program at the University of Texas after World War II, her intellect and imagination were hugely influenced by English literature, rather than German culture.

And, perhaps it was also the stories told at home by Aunt Inez's husband, Everett Shipplett, about his experiences as an Army dispatch rider (behind the trench-lines) in France during what was called, up to that time, The Great War, which informed her receptivity to the German professor's vaunting of the new Germany coming our way soon—too soon.

The next German—actually German-American-Texan—who was closer to Elizabeth's life than professor Heinrich was August (Oscar) Hein, who joined the Laredo Public Schools soon after the end of World War II. He had served in Patton's armored divisions engaged in the Battle of the Bulge in Belgium. He was the eldest son of a widow in Laredo, TX, and by 1949 the head man in a line-up of Hein brothers which put him in charge at the Hein family home.

A generation back, either Hein's father or grandfather had come to Texas from Germany. Oscar was a Rice Institute scholar and a football team member for the Rice Owls before World War II. It is not clear how well Elizabeth knew him in college.

1931

Class Recorder:
Anne Cornelius McCulloch
2348 Shakespeare Rd.
Houston, TX 77030

Elizabeth Nye Sorrell (B.A.) writes: "This is a time for reminiscing, especially about the war years, but my memory tonight is of the prewar years, 1930-31, when I was a senior at the Rice Institute. In the reserve library one day, I, a buxom lass in a red skirt and red wool jersey blouse, attracted the attention of one Heinrich Meyer, German professor. He was straight from the old country, wearing trousers that were European cut, suitable for high water, and a blonde haircut that stood straight up, very short.

Would I go dine with him at the Rice Hotel Roof? Attending Rice and working at the old Methodist Hospital on Tuam St., I had little time for dating, but I had never been to so glamorous a place as the Rice roof. "Yes," I replied, and the date was set. I remember he came for me at my aunt's home on Rice Boulevard in a taxi. For the important dinner date, I wore a swishy, green cocktail dress. Great fun! I would enjoy dining and dancing. It would be a memorable evening.

Aye, not so, for Dr. Heinrich Meyer was full of talk about Adolph Hitler, what a wonderful man he was! What a leader of the German people! How he was welding the youth into a great youth corps!

Yes, we dined, but we did not dance. I listened for hours. True, there was Houston, even then a sea of lights spread out over the prairie! No dancing, only "Hitler, heil Hitler!"

Shortly afterwards, I departed for my own pueblo on the Rio Grande to teach school for forty-eight years, trying to impart a love of Shakespeare I learned from Dr. Stockton Axson.

And now, sixty-four years later, I wonder what happened to Heinrich Meyer. Rumor had it that he married classmate Lois Reynolds Wright '32 (B.A.), and they lived in New Orleans during the war years. He held secret meetings in their apartment from which Lois was locked out. Soon he was suspected as a spy and interned for the duration. Whether this is true or not, I would like to be enlightened. Does anyone from the Class of 1931 know what happened to Heinrich Meyer?

And now I should like to add a word of praise for the *Sallyport*, which I find most interesting and the new format most attractive. I am grateful for Rice, which was the intellectual wellspring of my being! A great adventure of the spirit! *Gracias!*

Elizabeth's story published in the Rice alumni magazine describing Prof. Meyer's first date with Elizabeth, just before she graduated from Rice in 1930.

During his years as the professor of military science and tactics at Martin High School, then as assistant principal, he accompanied my mother (and me at about age ten) to high school football games at Shirley Field, west of the high school parking lot. There were other social events they attended together, but not too many. Elizabeth said several times, that she knew Hein's mother wouldn't let go of him in the Hein household, and besides, she would never convert to Roman Catholicism to meet the Hein family standards. As I look back, it seems odd, even, that the two ever came near forming "a personal relationship."

To hold a teaching position at Martin High was very much living in a goldfish bowl, where every nuance of a faculty member's behavior was under constant scrutiny by the school community on and off campus and by the Laredo Independent School District Board.

Elizabeth in her riding "habit."

An ingénue has returned to her hometown, 1931.

Her life after Rice Institute

The three women in the photo on page 58 were young school teachers. They were "best friends" from the early 1930s until after World War II had ended. In the author's childhood he experienced many "play times" at the Muller house, where there were three young children contemporaries of Elizabeth's toddler. Their mama, Julia Muller, and her husband, Adolf Furney Muller, were very close socially. The author's father, Norman Sorrell, the man wearing the dark hat and cardigan sweater, was employed by Muller in the business of crop factoring—buying farm crops up and down the length of rural Texas. Muller and several other local men sold crop purchase contracts forward—i.e., for future delivery to grocers, middle-men, and buyers of what must have been entire train-loads of produce, vegetables grown both near Laredo and down south, in the Rio Grande Valley.

This photo ("Gang of 5 hikers") identifies a group of five folks out in the wilderness in Webb County, on a hike on what I am guessing was A. Furney Muller's ranch (La Bota?). It's a social outing for three single school teacher ladies (or, one or two of the women might have been newlywed). The people in the photo, the Sam Taylor couple, and the A. F. Muller couple, were joined by Norman W. Sorrell and Alice Elizabeth Nye, who were dating, but not married yet.

Ruth Taylor (maiden name Ward) married a jewelry retail store operator who had stores in Laredo and Corpus Christi, TX. He was Sam Taylor. The firm was called Taylor Brothers Jewelers." The Ruth and Sam Taylor lived in Garland, Rockwall County, a suburb of Dallas. During this time Norman W. Sorrell (in about 1934) was in North Texas on a crop-buying trip. The circumstances furnished an elopement opportunity for Elizabeth and Norman. It was an excuse for my father and Elizabeth Nye to be out of town to be married. They eloped because his mother, the widow Irene H. Sorrell, had such emotional control over her oldest son that she could have stopped him from marrying—certainly if he and my mother were open to be married in Laredo, at home. Shortly after being widowed upon the death of Sterling Jobe Sorrell, Norman, the eldest son, resided with his mama in her digs at 1010 Corpus Christi Street, in Laredo.

The man who would have been Elizabeth's putative father-in-law, Sterling Jobe Sorrell, was born in Carter County, TN. He was in the U.S. Army, occupying Havana, Cuba. He married Irene Henrietta Barth-Martin Sorrell, a native of Charleston, SC, shortly after the war against Spain ended, while she was still a teenager.

Elizabeth hand-wrote names of the five photo subjects late in her eighties. It looks like she forgot who the photographer was—probably Adolph Furney Muller. Notice the photo taker stood in a place where his shadow would fall outside the field of vision for the shot. The long, narrow sticks of the hikers were most likely *carizzo*, which grows in shallow water or alluvial mud along the Rio Grande River.

SOCIETY BETWEEN SAN ANTONIO AND MEXICO

During the program known as "GI bill" for World War II veterans, or during the Korean War and the beginnings of the Cold War with the Soviet Union, Laredo on the north side of the river had a population of about 50,000. It had been a port of entry for international trade and banking between the United States and Mexico since 1840, more or less.

The social mores from 1898 and later? It was Mediterranean, South European, Roman Catholic, and, in politics, "blue dog" Democratic Party, progressive in social outlook. No one in South Texas was aware that there was actually a Republican Party in Texas, before the presidency of the Democrat, Harry S Truman. The "pols" were multi-cultural affiliates of *El Partido Viejo*, the "old party" in Webb and adjoining counties.

Eventual polite acceptance for a newcomer from north of the border in Webb County's social and economic milieu depended a lot on the newcomer's wealth and pedigree of his family in his place of origin. It helped if a migrant from the North or East was Roman Catholic. It was smart for the "new" people to be docile, compliant in not presenting opposition to stakeholders who bore *El Partido Viejo* or its standard bearers.

Alice Elizabeth, born on the farm in Webb County, her grandfather, T. C. Nye, having for two decades "gotten-along" in town, and Grandpa Nye, having had skill in the ways and wiles of the border people, were not really "carpetbaggers." The first families and the adjacent tier of Webb county bourgeois were a part of Alice Elizabeth's fabric in childhood. As a young person and later, her life-long friends, neighbors, and colleagues in the local schools in which she had been a pupil. That same cohort after her Rice University education were well within her comfort level. She loved them. She would tell you that she loved them. They were all *her* people—even the very few who found her to be a little outspoken or overly dramatic as a classroom teacher.

A few competitive spirits around Martin High School may have been envious of her self-assuredness. Having written material as a cub reporter for the *Laredo Times* daily paper as a teenager gave her the legs it took to navigate Laredo and Webb County as it was in the decades of the '20s through the 1940s. This was good, because a lot had gone sour for the local Nye family between 1890 and 1938. It didn't seem to rub off on her. Turning back to the subject of mores or culture between San Antonio, Texas, and Mexico, it is useful to make some comparisons of the area with other paradigms.

For one example, what is it about Larry McMurtry's *Lonesome Dove* that has a deep similarity in its early settlers from both north and south of the river, with Elizabeth's world of 1909 to 2007? The world as it was when Grandfather T. C. Nye and his family lived briefly in Cotulla to settle sixty miles further south, prior to the beginning of the twentieth century, was very much like the *Lonesome Dove* world.[7] Alice Elizabeth's roots had carried DNA of the Nyes from Sandwich, MA. The family members, or some of them, in *Tejas* had adapted to someone like the fellow you see (following page) surveying cattle on his horse. An adaptation such as this cowboy represents was forged in the teenage years of the orphan life of T. C. Nye in Matagorda, aided by the Matagorda folks, and aided by his nanny, Mrs. Harvey, and by the Christ Church community; and, even by Shanghai Pierce. The Texas border with Mexico takes a flavor of the Third World one glimpses in Humphrey Bogart's Casablanca nightclub in the film of the same name. Think also of *The African Queen*.

Many variants of those themes are repeated in the towns on the south bank of the Rio Grande River, from Brownsville/Reynosa northwest toward El Paso, TX, and its partner city, Ciudad Juarez.

Generic Texas 19th century cowboy. (Photo courtesy Library of Congress.)

The still active writer, Tom Miller authored *On the Border*, subtitled "Portraits of America's Southwestern Frontier," published in 1981 by Harper & Row. Also, here, in the midst of our own personal comments about the modern local culture of Alice Elizabeth Nye's community, are perhaps snippets (in quotation) which I use here to describe aspects of social life "available" to visitors to Nuevo Laredo. I fear this is too candid because of the seaminess portrayed by Miller is far from strait-laced. Nor is the part of our tale in consonance with puritanical roots of Alice Elizabeth Nye and her family. And, yet, there they are—two worlds north and south of the Rio Grande, in a not-so-sharp contrast. Unfortunately, one of the girl's closest family strayed far from puritannical roots of even his forefathers.

Miller quotes Graham Greene's own comments about Laredo in Greene's book *Another Mexico*: "Oh, life, that begins on the other side. And so, I crossed over to find life." Miller continues:

"My guide was Joe Harmes, a local reporter. Our first mission in Nuevo Laredo was to find Carlos, who by day, was an instructor at Laredo Junior College and who, by night, was a crazed and serious bar-hopper. Carlos was the embodiment of borderland brilliance, a backsliding philosophic *sabelotodo* (know-it-all) who reduced the world to a belch while pontificating on its problems. 'Just meet me in Nuevo Laredo,' he exclaimed when we tried to plan. 'Where?' we asked. 'You'll find me. Ask around.'

"We drove up Guerrero Street stopping at different bars until we got to La Cava. Carlos was sitting at a booth on the far wall waving his arms about, making an existential point about dope-dealing. His companions were two Anglos from Laredo and a Nuevo Laredo friend. In the space of twenty minutes Carlos managed to conquer all South America, dissolve the Catholic church, and corner the black market on every conceivable herb.

"Soon the party spilled into the street where we split up into two cars. A friend was attending a wedding reception at the Club Leones and we agreed to meet there. As we were about to pull away, Carlos walked over. 'Listen you ... *chingados*,' he whispered furtively. 'I can't bring these guys with me. I don't know how much more of them I can take ... He glanced across the street at his passengers—'it's Christian versus pagan, and the guys have no idea what it's like to be a pagan. Let me dump these Christians ... I'll meet you at the reception.'

"Carlos aimed his car toward the border while we drove off to the Club Leones filled with five hundred drinking and dancing celebrants in elegant evening gowns and tuxedos. We found our friend just as the bride was tossing her flowers to the women clustered about her. The upper crust of Nuevo Laredo and Laredo society was in attendance.

"Earlier in the day Gary Payne, manager of the Laredo Chamber of Commerce, had explained the social levels. 'It's like fifteenth-century England, the way people are aware of their class on the border,' he said. 'In Laredo the high class doesn't recognize the low class. A middle class is developing, but it is still very small.'

"Laredo, like many other Texas communities, was for generations run under the patrón system in which elections, salaries, employment, law, and order are controlled by one family. Laredo's mayor and patrón had been Pepe Martin, who in 1978 was convicted on federal mail fraud charges. As the Martin dynasty crumbled, the Sanchez family, which had been in the typewriter repair business, struck oil on leased land. Once the Sanchezes were millionaires, they became a force to rival the Martins, investing their newfound wealth in banks and a daily newspaper.

" 'The Sanchez family is one of the very few which has gone from one class to the other,' Gary Payne went on. 'Years ago, Tony Sanchez, Jr., wanted to marry one of the Martin girls, and that just couldn't happen because of the class system. That's one of the reasons they set up the Laredo News—so they could get back at the Martins.'

"At the wedding reception another custom was taking place—the groom was stripped of his jacket, shoes, and socks, hoisted upon the shoulders of spirited friends, and carried around the room. On stage a nine-piece band in matching blue leisure suits blared out enough of a melody to satisfy every taste from disco to waltz. 'At Mexican weddings,' Joe shouted over the din, 'the number of people doesn't indicate the number of friends the bride and groom have, as much as the number of relatives. The father of the bride is somber because of his investment in the reception. The mother is concerned about the old man's drunkenness. The groom's parents are usually the only ones at the head table having a good time. It's not like small village weddings where the in-laws get to eat the goat while the rest of the guests settle for the leftovers. Here, everything is on the bride's father."

"The wedding fiesta would go well into the night, and Joe insisted we had more important things to do than wait for Carlos. 'We're off to Boys Town' . . . He wasn't after sexual favors, he insisted, he simply loved the ambience . . .

"Joe's favorite spot was the Marabú, one of the classier establishments in the zona. Outside were parked Cadillacs, pickups, Winnebagos, Volkswagens, and horses. Inside the Marabú was a Formica wonderland of plastic plants and speckled walls. An elevated dance floor was circled by tables and booths, with a bar next to the door. The jukebox played 'Macho Man' relentlessly but no one ever danced. Waiters scurried about serving drinks.

"Over the years Nuevo Laredo's zona roja has earned a reputation as a playpen for University of Texas fraternity boys and state legislators. The evening I visited, oil hands, truckers, salesmen, ranchers, cops, and students filled the Marabú, attracted by prostitutes who were alternately hostile and shy, aggressive and submissive."[8]

The Miller narration shows us a party of men at a Laredo bar in about the year 1981 at a late hour. The bar was named, "La Cava"; the men decamp from the bar for another event, a wedding reception including 500 guests at the Nuevo Laredo "Lion's Club."

Miller's account of his nighttime party-hopping in Nuevo Laredo is here cut short due to our certainty that readers do not need the full account of Miller's and friends' escapades in the brothel and bar called The Marabú. We do not need the "full Monty" in order to provide colorful insights into the culture and social mores typical of most border towns that line the south banks of the Rio Grande between Tijuana, at the Pacific coast, to the mouth of the Rio Grande river at Brownsville, Texas.

Here are a few final words of reflection on the visitors to Nuevo Laredo, Mexico, from the United States: Look where "we" have been in this story. From Norse raiders of Lindisfarne in 780 A.D. to "gringos" slumming in Nuevo Laredo. It has made progress over the years of history? Really?

RAYMOND & TIRZA MARTIN HIGH SCHOOL–1937

The single most pivotal relationship for Elizabeth (lasting years from about 1951 through 2007) was a star pupil, editor of the "La Pitahaya" yearbook and news journal who became a professional journalist as editor of the *Laredo Morning Times*. He is Odilon Arambula, who was also a high school classmate of this author.

"Odi" was one of a few who appeared to pay respects to Mrs. Sorrell at committal of her ashes to a Laredo grave-site in July 2007. He has also passed into eternity since the writing of this biography started in 2015. Odi's influence was crucial to the planned launch of this biography, as were Mr. Bill Green and the President of the Texas A & M University, Mr. Ray Keck.

Odilon's presence in the 1950s and his work were celebrated daily in Room 250, side-by-side with Elizabeth in the assembly and layout of the high school yearbook for most of Odi's years at Martin High School. His collaboration with Elizabeth's journalistic contributions to *The Laredo Morning Times* from about 1960 through her continued writings up to 2007 made him virtually a member of Elizabeth's family over the forty-seven years—nearly five decades—of Elizabeth's teaching and journalism careers until her very end in 2007.

This biography of Elizabeth Nye Sorrell could not have had as substantial a foundation without Mr. Arambula's guiding presence in her lifetime. His affection for her is set forth in the column Odi wrote at the time of the lady's birthday in 2006, after she had retired to The Meadows facility in San Antonio, TX. The verve displayed in Odi's column about Elizabeth says it all about the relationship he enjoyed as "captain" of her team of colleagues. It is repeated in full scope here:

MONDAY WASH

A Laredo legend named Elizabeth Sorrell

See article transcription on page 109

I quote again a part of Odilon's account of the origins of the Martin High building project in late 1930s:

"Thereafter the newspaper published another article by Miss Nye, an essay on the need to expand and improve school curriculum, listing courses in the language arts . . .

"The principal took notice, the superintendent took notice, the school board took notice and heard from the advocates who agreed with the young woman. . . . It planted the seed that meant, within the next decade, Laredo would have a brand-new, state-of-the-art high school—Raymond and Tirza Martin High School."

Until about 1955, you who are not familiar with Laredo and Webb County must see that Raymond & Tirza Martin High, opened in 1937, was a jewel in Laredo's crown among public educational institutions of any level. As is the case in many small Texas towns, it was the platform for local football and other sports teams, such as basketball. It was a fount of the town's cherished college-bound put forward into the world just before World War II. Several excellent Catholic secondary schools had been in operation prior to 1937, but their numbers were smaller in graduates.

The main entry facade of Martin High, as it appeared in 2015.

Martin High was the platform, if you will, for the classroom-staged performances of Elizabeth in a forty-nine-year career teaching English Literature, while after normal class hours supervising the production of a yearbook ("La Pitahaya") and the school's own news journal. Also, after school hours during the 1950s, Elizabeth intensified year-to-year her social news column and photo-journalist contributions to the *Laredo Morning Times* (now a Hearst Corporation affiliate) and two additional weekly newspapers, *The South Texas Citizen* and later *La Re Dos*. Her assignments came from publishers Billy Hall (the *Citizen*) and Meg Guerrra (*La Re Dos*). Local politics was documented in all three local newspapers. Attendance at most civic and social functions to cover events was a mandate, a given condition, for this woman widowed several years back. She also personally performed photo-journalism for the Martin High yearbook, through nine months of the school year, but routinely carried a camera along to all civic and social events she covered for her daily and weekly newspaper publishers.

Exposure of this lady in the role of, say, Shakespeare and major-poets teacher and an *empresario* of reportage for 70 years (if we do not include her reporting of sports events in her Old High pre-college years) in the same community from 1934 through almost 2006.

It made her a well known, highly regarded personality over several generations on the north side of the river for all those years, unbroken by almost any other distractions (except her ten-year marriage and the birth of one child as the only major distractions). It now amuses us that until her widowhood, her husband insisted she not learn to drive the two-door pre-War black Ford sedan, which was as much the husband's baby as was the child he knew for six years.

Martin High was the focal point of many Laredo events and initiatives. With Laredo's school board membership of powerful men, it was further the focal point for all of Alice Elizabeth Nye Sorrell's associations, friendships, and social activity for her entire life after Norman Sorrell's death in 1944. She "knew" everybody of high and low estate, and they all regarded her as part of the local landscape in a friendly way. Education in Texas, yearbook and reporting work, and her master's degree research and writing at Austin 1947-48 expanded her circle of colleagues statewide.

Her sphere of contacts and influence was multiplied by business people from both Nuevo Laredo and the Texas side, court and state politicians, legislative officers, and elected office-holders. But her sphere was magnified even more by people of all social stations who had firsthand exposure to her recitations over five decades as an inspired English lit teacher and a cultural advocate for all cultures of the prior 1,180 years of history in the books by the year 1980 AD.

What made her an advocate of such scope at that time and place? Why would she adopt "advocacy" of who she was and who her people had been before 1931? There is similarity between the circumstances attending the Norse invasions, settlement, and domestication in Britain, at one level, to the religious and Adam-Smith-dissent-with-revolution convulsions in the British archipelago. Merely being dissenters exploded into their taking ship and striking out to grasp *Lebensraum* in the New World, free of dominance by English government social stratification and the English church. Elizabeth and Grandpa Nye continued the family traditions.

She felt her intellectual roots in history as a Nye descendant from Sandwich, MA. That was in resonance with the Nye family history reaching to the conquests of Norse and Viking tribes, encompassing a 2,000-year evolution of the English language all over the globe.

This anecdote adds insight upon the lady's independent spirit: Quickly after Norman Sorrell's death in the summer of 1944, Elizabeth persuaded her friend, Ruth Taylor, to instruct her in the Ford stick gear-shift and clutch operation. Elizabeth, the widow, gained much more freedom of movement and involvement in school and community day-in and day-out. She disposed of (by cash sale) a hoard of deer rifles and shotguns (quail and dove) which Norman had assembled over a fifteen-year period—one might call the guns her spousal "insurance death benefit proceeds." The guns were *all* Norman left her.

The daily and weekend pursuit of interviews and photos of event attendees continued for her entire life, until she moved to occupy her granddaughter's home. She then went to The Meadows retirement residence in San Antonio. Even then in 2005 and 2006 Elizabeth composed and submitted a few columns of copy for a major San Antonio newspaper, *The Express News*.

STRUGGLE AND FAMILY ANECDOTES 1944 –1949

Elizabeth's life changed due to a final illness and death in May 1944 of her spouse. He occupied a hospital bed in the darkened main salon of Grampa Nye's homestead at 1706 Farragut St. as his heart failure progressed to the end. This is now is from the viewpoint of the 5 year-old child who was at home on the May afternoon, playing alone in the front yard as the death of his father occurred. He was they thought in the care of the *criada, Maria de los Angeles Zuniga.* Late on the sunny May afternoon he is still alone, left, the only child to be brought up by a single school teacher mother, then aged about thirty five, who never remarried. But, single parent and full-time teacher, was she adequate to this. to the challenges of single parenthood? Elizabeth's mother-in-law, and even more certainly Elizabeth's sister-in-law, Madonna S. Teller, did not think so. They were vocal in their disapproval of Elizabeth's role as parent and full-time school teacher for several years after 1944.

The immediate family Sorrells (who survived Norman W.A. Sorrell) younger brother Hazen, a Navy enlistee, and the Freeman Teller couple, were childless. They lived upper middle-class lifestyles; the Tellers were outspoken in suggesting the child ("little Sonny") be sent away from Laredo and his mother to be educated else-where, a military prep school, probably to Allen Academy at Bryan-College Station. The well-off Tellers in Houston were driven by a sense of deep disapproval of the very essence of Alice Elizabeth, given their cultural background and prejudices this was quite natural. By this time Elizabeth had a 15 year history in Martin High School, and she really knew who she was. She had now attained practice in "roaring" in her deep, well projected voice in classroom 250. Neither the Tellers, nor anyone else in the world grasped with accuracy just *how sure, and sure-footed,* Elizabeth (as she was known publicly, without the "Alice") had become.

To say the Sorrell family had no clue just what they were dealing with in their frontal charge to remove the child from Elizabeth was like bargaining with a live tiger for her hide!! Elizabeth's fury was scarcely contained in her feelings and responses to this matter. She was mad as hell!! Bewilderment overcame the boy-child who was the focal point of all the adult disputations. He felt *alone* in any event, and the family bad feelings made for even more isolation in an emotional sense.

The mood hung in the air about 1706 Farragut over the boy's head like residual tear gas which was wafted by breeze from a nearby riot after the antagonists had spent their ammunition. It was said the "obvious" inadequacy of the "poor," single, widowed mother made her unfit to be a mother. The writer remembers harsh speeches all around the houses visited by Madonna Teller in behalf of sending the candidate for exile, off to be rescued, to be made "a man." Anything but Elizabeth, they said. Grandmother Irene and uncle Hazen and his lovely spouse, Mary-Frank were all caught in-between the vitriol expended. Elizabeth vented no vitriolic reaction, even if mostly non-verbal.

It was Elizabeth's raw, outspoken independence to meet all challenges in life not just in the classroom; her competitive nature was stoked.

The teaching and administrative staff social structure of Raymond and Tirza Martin High School could feel and see this new reality of their "colleague". She was fired-up. It was her devotion to arts, including poetry, literature and the humanistic ideals of modernism that the culture had set for a stage to be wholly within Elizabeth's keen grasp by 1945. It was fanatical devotion to her pupils (i.e., her "public") and the young people's culturally diverse families of less-than-complete-Anglo-configuration; the people of Laredo, the whole of what Laredo's culture had stood for was alien to the Tellers, in particular. Hazen Sorrell and family kept a civil demeanor to life in Laredo as public employees. They never dreamed of "fighting city hall", a two-century old monument on the north bank of the Rio Grande. City Hall was the cockpit of the very people which the Tellers (or the Sorrells ?) thought to be "unwashed." This portrait of *realpolitic* and her Rice education in her preoccupation with the liberal arts since the "enlightenment" made of Alice Elizabeth a *she-bear* who recited poetry, as she laid-into the archenemies of her ideals. It led to ego, and it made for Elizabeth to prevail in all things, on all stages where performance was due. She never uttered judgments—pejoratives—upon the larger Texas or United States social experiment.

An aphorism—an eighteenth century motto—could be applied now, derived, founded on the facts we relate above. One of the appropriates is the motto of the City of Paris: *"She is tossed by waves but does not sink."* This has been around as a Latin aphorism in literature since 1358. Looking at the travails for merest survival of Grampa Nye, seeing the Nye clan immigrants "on trek", and recalling the Nye religious dissenters from before the days of the Danish invasions of Britain, it may be the mettle in the Danish genes and nurture of centuries of immigration westward that set the lady's metal in a mold.

She endured World War II like a person longing to be posted to Crimea like Florence Nightingale had she been confined to England.

She barely endured the volatile temperament of a little son who tended, in pre-teen years, to demand his way, and who damned all other constraints. She was driven to a new resource in the boy's pre-puberty life, a fancy female PhD. child psychologist!!

Here is an anecdote out of really cold winter in Laredo in about 1947 or 1948 which illustrates Elizabeth's willing, sanguine spirit: Porfirio Flores, Sheriff of Webb County and her former classroom pupil, called early one evening. It was about a little boy held in jail custody, a runaway from another state. He had been out in the weather, on the road for quite a while. The jail was a tough place. He asked her if she would take the boy, feed and house him at least overnight. The Webb County jail was not a decent place to put a child so young. Her response was "yes," bring him over to 1706 Farragut.

The boy was caked with dry dirt. His eyes shone out like he had been done up in minstrel's cake makeup. She fed him well, after first sticking his body in a claw-foot tub of hot water. She sat on a low stool and, with a brush, vigorously went over every inch of him - skin and all his crevices- so hard that the kid said "ouch."

I watched this from the next room. For sure, there were times when Elizabeth was for no nonsense. Anyone who needed a scrubbing (including me, the resident waif) got it. Her tone of voice when projecting into a classroom was full, almost baritone, never sounding soprano, nor alto nor tenor. She projected herself. Though not quite abrasive, that voice *commanded one's attention*. When it was poetry, they listened. When it was the soliloquy of Hamlet or the burble of the witches in Act I of Macbeth.

She did not consciously intend to portray the Red Queen from Lewis Carroll's *Through the Looking Glass*. A Phyllis Diller imitator she was not. It would be interesting to have been there to see the impact of "Off with their heads!" The little runaway from Webb County lockup? She thought nothing of her intervention, at all.

Graduate school education at UT 1947-1948, leading to an M.A.

Was it only a higher salary that motivated Elizabeth to enter a Master's degree in English program at U T in Austin? But later Dean Harry Ransom, the celebrated academician, was her tutor for her Master's thesis in the subject matter of the poet Robert Browning and his contemporaries. The thesis was to be a survey of texts or critical commentaries on late Victorian-era poets, parsing the works and comparing them. I doubt such work came to any engineer-like conclusions. It was accepted by Dr. Ransom. She was awarded the Master's in Fine Arts. The thesis was shelved-away in the stacks at the University of Texas main campus library. But we were told that someone who had un-shelved the bound book, and it was never re-shelved. No tissue copies (from the days of old Royal keystroke non-electric machines) exist. Her Master's is framed, housed with one of her grandchildren.

Much came out of her scholarship in the Victorian poets. John Keats and Percy Bysshe Shelley were quoted around and about, both in classes and in casual conversations after hours. Her zeal her poetic nerve flowered, reflected in her Room 250 classroom on the west side of Martin High School. So adept was she at making Beowulf listenable to twelfth grade pupils from homes where Spanish is spoken, this teacher somehow gilded literature with sufficient panache to graft memory and recollection of the names of the poets in hundreds of her senior class students, after about 1949.

What has been said here was feedback (a lot within earshot of the author) from hundreds of onetime Laredo public school alumni given to Elizabeth in her many forays into the salons of Texas for wedding receptions and reunions of various kinds over the years after her retirement. These seances went on all over the map, in hundreds of venues where Laredo High alumni gathered to celebrate family and civic occasions, whether in Laredo, San Antonio, Houston, Dallas, or Washington, D.C.

THE WAR'S IMPACT

The War dominated civilian life in Laredo, TX, from Pearl Harbor onward, much as in other small North American towns that became important to the war effort. Those of us at least eighty years of age remember the ever-present weight on our shoulders—that feeling of dread. Until about Christmas of 1944 or by May 1945, no one knew we were actually winning!

Small towns like Laredo grew rapidly as hundreds of thousands of men were mobilized and sent to all points for training. In Laredo the rapid pouring of concrete runways for an Army air base began in 1942. It is estimated the population of Laredo in 1945, was near 39,000.

Added to food and tire rationing, the draft had a severe emotional impact on Laredo's schools, particularly Martin High and a few other private schools that declined due to the volunteers or draft of many hundreds of local males of draft age. After 1943, during months of training and deployment of our boys to the Pacific and to Europe, came telegrams to families that their sons or husbands were missing in action, captured, or killed in battle. Confrontations between German and U.S. troops accelerated in late 1943 into 1944, particularly after June 6, 1944.

Home atmosphere during the War

Recall, Elizabeth was at Room 250 8 a.m. to 6 p.m. The child and the *criada* (maid/nursemaid) held at Grandpa's house. In the homestead at 1706 Farragut Street, the dark polished-wood Philco radio in the sitting room was tuned to Mexican news and music presentations in daylight hours, for the entertainment of a *criada*. By supper time, it was tuned to news broadcasts in English covering—what else?—the War. The *criadas* employed in Elizabeth's household, in T. C. Nye's home, were Nuevo Laredo residents who commuted over the international bridge for employment on the Texas side of the River.

We will see one house maid really was *majordomo* in the Sorrell and Nye families' homes for several decades. *Criadas* were very important as daytime nannies to more than one generation of related children. They were even shared or spread out over interlocking extended families. They became to all intents and purposes the *majordomos* who ran the households and carried out duties of butler and cook, among other roles. Recall the character of Liza Doolittle in *My Fair Lady*; then you grasp what a *criada* meant in Texas in the early and mid-twentieth centuries. These ladies were not slaves in Pharaoh's Egypt.

Elizabeth remained at the Martin High School building until two or three hours after classes ended for supervision of the "La Pitahaya" staff's production, design, assembly on drawing board, and the writing of graphic content for the yearbook. It was assembled in Room 250 immediately after a day and some evenings of school events that had taken place, usually that very week. There being only one automobile in the Sorrell family until May 1944, Elizabeth was (in getting to or from the school) dependent on catching a ride with another faculty member, or rarely, from a student who had a vehicle for transportation. Webb County was a farming and ranching community, so some high school young people had access to trucks due to their family's farm, ranch, or other business.

What did the Martin High English Lit pupils and "La Pitahaya" staffs think about the war atmosphere? Remember, the majority of the school census was of Mexican descent, from families that may have been on the Texas side of the river since before 1845. This author remembers blatant discrimination practiced by Caucasians more than one hundred miles north of the Rio Grande in Texas against indigenous Indian, Mexican, Negro, mulatto, and all non-Aryan races. We heard about this, but never saw it in Laredo, proper. Imagine this: Our Laredo north-of-the-river boys of all backgrounds fighting and dying for America in all theaters of the global war. Elizabeth's cousin, Randall Nye, a son of "Pinkie" Nye and his *mestizo* wife, Ozema Gutierrez, went from a Laredo High classroom to Texas A & M for a short time, then into the Army Air Corps, where he served in India and Burma.

Public records show many Mexican-descent citizen soldiers in the armed forces were volunteers, not conscripts. Many were from the classes of 1937 to 1939 right into the thick of the war, all Martin High pupils of Elizabeth Nye Sorrell. The cultural history of a North American and British culture had been proclaimed in literature in Martin High, not just taught, in Room 250 by Elizabeth. She taught the heritage going back—going further behind—northern migrants to *Tejas* of the prior one hundred years, they, who carried migrant genes imported in North European bodies cum North Americans.

A foundation of blended local values, for which Laredo and south Texas stood, like melting pot lore of North America, from inception, swept down through *Tejas*, from 1836. And, it came right at us—we who lived in the twentieth century on the border; including so many whose genetic heritage lay far to the south of the Rio Grande.

Muffled echoes of German (Axis) racial sentiment in Texas, which originated from before 1917, and the isolationism felt by American progressive, socialist/leftists in economic depression years did not show up in Webb County, insofar as we can personally recall from daily experience and what we got in daily newspapers. Certainly Elizabeth would have been acutely alert to such issues, had they existed. Pro-Axis sentiments did not dare crawl into the light of day in Webb County, Texas, after December 1941, and least of all from Hispanic people or their grandparents. Pearl Harbor's shock was a rap in the chops, broadcasting that we must fight, or we would not thereafter survive as we were, and had been.

Olive to brown-complexioned, *mestizo*, and non-Caucasian people had been "on the land," occupying regions north of Rio Grande (up to about the thirty-seventh parallel of latitude) of years prior to 1700. Some of my dearest friends in the Finchum family of Tennessee would here chide me for ignoring the real native-Americans ("Indians") who had been on all the lands for thousands of years before any Europeans sailed west.

No overnight influx of military personnel or others involved in construction or support for the war effort was visible until later in 1942. The author recalls a visit to a teacher-colleague of Elizabeth in a residential area south of the new air base. Elizabeth saw yellow-and-blue fuselages take off to the south over the Rio Grande. (When she saw the aircraft ascend, Elizabeth was most likely at the home of the Lemoine family in the newest eastern home development, gaping into the sky not far from the new base.) Later in the war, training activity involved B-17 crew gunnery training flights, where an orange-painted fighter towed a long sleeve of material behind to permit the sleeves to be targeted by the gunners who we thought might be preparing for bombing in Europe.

Alice Elizabeth Nye a widow

Elizabeth became a widow on 17 May 1944. A heart defect diagnosed in late 1943 worked congestive heart failure's course for Norman Sorrell in the main, darkened salon of Grandfather T. C. Nye's house. Nurses flowed in and out, Elizabeth continued her regular school routines, and the family lost a salary check for Norman's service in the county tax office. She may have felt trepidation; the extended family and the six-year-old son did not see a quibble from the woman between formal diagnosis and this death. To all she seemed stoic, quiet, maybe eyes downcast. Her real grieving came in months and years after.

The husband and father's death meant Air Corps sergeants (who had three-plus stripes and a wife) could rent bedrooms or a few remodeled apartments with kitchens and baths. There were more soldiers, dozens by late 1943, and over-full barracks. A wing and a spare bedroom in Grandfather Nye's old house were let to two sergeants with wives. To cleanse after the death of the Sorrell husband, the sergeants applied pastel wall paint to wood and plaster in the house, not a simple chore because it had sixteen-foot ceilings and 1900s-era frosted gas chandeliers, re-wired for electricity.

Alice Elizabeth Sorrell responded to air raid sirens on June 6, 1944—the day of the famous D-Day landings in Normandy, France. She circulated to assure all that "we think the landings may be going forward," and some one of us small ones looked sleepily out of the bay window facing south, framing a bright moon in a blue-black, cloudless sky looking down on the Mexican border.

Martin High School students and teaching staff in 1944 heard increasing reports of Laredo High alumni war casualties. A few of the young 1940 and 1941 students who had volunteered stood out, in notable deaths. Handwritten letters were posted by boys on active duty to Alice Elizabeth Nye at school. A ritual of the war years, in addition to

Savings Bond sales rallies, was the civic-music-association classical orchestra events; artists were presented in the Martin High gymnasium of evenings. Some ballet, many choirs, and some "pop" artists came, but most memorably, one of the several field bands of the Red Army of the Soviet Union, toured with a cast of dancing Russian, or Cossack, military men. These Russians showed rousing athleticism; they beguiled an audience with their power.

EMPTY NEST–1955

The teaching of English classes and the assembly of the "La Pitahaya" yearbook gave full life to Elizabeth and immediate family. She enjoyed the fall of 1952 all the way through the spring of 1955 because she shared those days more closely and collegially with her only son because he became a part of her daily routine more than ever as a pupil at Martin High. The Korean War was not neatly ended, so parents and high school pupils were all concerned about a military draft. The mindset of everyone included preparation for the young people's acceptance of enlistment in a branch of the services after secondary education was done or matriculation into colleges or, increasingly after 1946, both avenues—whereby young high school graduates could join Reserve Officers Training programs not only in high schools, but in almost all colleges and universities.

So, it was for Elizabeth and family, the boy being in high school Army ROTC and planning application for fall 1955 entry into a Naval ROTC program at Rice University, Elizabeth's alma mater back in 1931.

Wars only mildly preoccupied the Nyes in Laredo from 1917 to 1919.

Then onset of German military expansion in 1934 occupied Elizabeth's consciousness only peripherally from 1931 through 1940. But then dire circumstances of war were imposed in 1941–1945. The Cold War and Korean conflicts between "The West" and Marxist-Leninist political powers followed very closely on the heels of the formal end of World War II. Such wars-ended allowed only a short breath of peace, with demobilization in the fall of 1945.

It didn't seem to the people of Laredo, TX, and to Martin High faculty and student body that the "Iron Curtain" speech of Sir Winston Churchill on March 5, 1946, was anywhere but "under the radar"—that is, until in 1950 news of the world began to focus on a potential and then actual military invasion of South Korea. Before the end of June 1950, it was "here we go again . . ." accompanied by disbelief in the U.S. hinterlands, the boondocks between coasts.

Winston Church delivering *Sinews of Peace,* his "Iron Curtain" speech at Westminster College, Fulton, Missouri on Mar 5, 1946. (Photo courtesy of Westminster College.)

A photo of Winston Churchill speaking at Westminster College in Fulton, MO, shows President Harry S Truman, in cap and gown, sitting behind the podium where the British hero stood with drollery delivering the gravest of news that had never been anticipated by his Fulton audience. It took years for the Iron Curtain image to sink in in Texas. That terror was imposed upon Laredo, TX, with the first aluminum corpse transfer cases being brought in with Laredo boys for burial. By then Martin High boys under age eighteen in the ROTC unit were invited to put together a squad armed with World War II-era rifles to go to the cemetery on a sunny day to fire volleys over the graves when taps were played by a bugler from the American Legion post.

Alice Elizabeth Nye Sorrell's world had changed in a way her cohort could not have anticipated before 1946 or 1947—what was going down was the clear prospect of another generation of sons born in Webb County in jeopardy of having to fight in large numbers in foreign wars. Complacency of ordinary citizens nationwide that was palpable in 1914 was thirty-six years later being crushed with fresh physical and emotional wounds that reached to every family in all little towns and villages in Texas and the nation, including Webb County and Laredo.

The seriousness of all of Elizabeth's pupils' plans to go into the military, at the level it had been experienced for a full decade beginning in 1939, grew in the people at Martin High School—it became pervasive in all high schools and colleges. It was so much a part of day-to-day reality for ordinary people, they went about life planning to be shot at and planning to shoot back. South Texas is and always has been a place where rifles, side-arms, and shotguns were at close hand. In 1836—and for the next hundred-plus years—weapons were simply the way families got their white-tail deer meat and wild turkeys during hunting season.

All of that was part of the "back story" of Elizabeth's world for the first forty-one years of her life as a widow with a single child to raise while she watched out her window from Room 250 when the bands practiced and the ROTC drilled regularly. For the fledgling about to vacate the nest of the single-parent teacher, it was a world of anticipation of going away. The meaning of going was cemented to the military as a virtual new home for the newly fledged.

Her interest in social column writing—and the necessary social life to go with the reporting—had grown stronger and had been the subject of talk with her newspaper publisher friends through the period of life after her husband's death in 1944. To be the widow who now could drive the family car and get about town freely was independence she could have now (but not before her husband's death). She had freedom. The fledgling was going out on his own, so to speak—no daily supervision by the parent. Being so independent in spirit, her new freedom and prospect of the empty nest just increased her relish for life after May of 1955. It also signaled she could sell the Nye family homestead on Farragut Street, distribute proceeds to all of T. C. Nye's descendants and pick a smaller, more manageable duplex or apartment for her shelter. No need to plan—to make a permanent home for the fledgling—once he was fledged.

ELIZABETH'S ALLOTTED TIME FROM 1989–2006

After the party is over, it is frequently said the "after party" may still be about to rekindle festivities. Just where is the fun happening? If a career of many years becomes telescoped into one or two-year-long lasting parties, the spectral thought of inactivity, settling into dotage, is no fun to contemplate. For the sixteen-year period after 1989, Elizabeth had attained her eightieth birthday and lived in a modest apartment in the 1800 block of Laredo Street. Yes, physical slowdown pulled a shade on a dramatic personality. But she felt close to her Laredo friends. Nevertheless, she continued a social life of sorts, circumscribed by diminution, then loss, of ability to drive an automobile.

Readers who are now "of a certain age"—especially if you were pupils of Elizabeth at Martin High School or part of the Christ Church Episcopal on Lane Avenue—may have seen her at social events or at church. Or perhaps she was shopping for her groceries at the HEB store on Corpus Christi St., and you offered her a ride home around the corner. She had walked several blocks down Laredo Street to approach her grocery location. She crossed Corpus Christi at some peril.

Her family 900 miles distant in every direction became aware she was riskily navigating on foot for banking errands. And now she was in danger from traffic, a gradual weakening of her vision and reflexes, sorely tested by those visits to the bank or teacher's credit union.

Elizabeth made only one trip by air to Colorado Springs, CO, in the early '90s, for several days to visit in company of this author and his then social friend, Myrene Hoge. From 1961 forward, Alice Elizabeth Nye Sorrell would not consider living any place other than the town where she was born, to which she had committed well before 1930. Her bond was absolute. Only one adult child had been away since 1955; well, that was just too bad.

Several times a year from 1995 through 2001, Ms. Hoge and this writer took flights for four-day holidays in Laredo. On these junkets we were all occupied following the social columnist's very busy social circuit to parties and events in Laredo.

Ensconced in the wedding receptions and constant parties—of course, note-pad and camera in hand—Elizabeth continued her lifelong *métier* in note taking, pocketing remarks like little prizes, the warmest of greetings from hundreds of former pupils, their extended family, friends, and colleagues. On almost all those visits Elizabeth's grandson and/or granddaughter came to town and accompanied her on her social "rounds," sometimes three or four events per weekend.

The most remarkable event for Elizabeth and her family was a Laredo civic center banquet, sponsored by the *Laredo Morning Times* and one of the banks, where the guest of honor on the dais this time was none-other than Elizabeth, herself. This big event was to announce and present a scholarship fund for worthy local graduates of a new high school for the arts. The fund was named in honor of Elizabeth, in recognition of her service to educational and social communities over several decades, including her journalism forays on behalf of the *Laredo Times* and two separate weekly publications that printed her society columns most weeks since her formal retirement from teaching in the summer of 1979. The civic center event (see photos in Appendix 1) brought all of Elizabeth's immediate family—son, adult grandchildren, even the author's former wife, mother of the Elizabeth Nye Sorrell descendants—to Laredo to celebrate her taking bows in "celebrity." In many ways this was the pinnacle of her life, owing to citywide publicity and an outpouring of civic adulation in joyful honor of the lady before, during, and after the event proper. Her Victorian dramatics of poem phrase and a sharp humor never ceased to inspire laughter.

These socials showed phenomena experienced by and among showbiz, academic, journalistic, publicist, and political cohorts all over these United States. Red carpet treatments and TV news talking heads (of Texas and the nation) show that the beautiful people in public life do "take care of their own." When the kudos that Elizabeth had been serving up for decades within society at large came around for her, the lionizer enjoyed her turn for her rewards.

This author observed for seventy years a regular, pulsating swirl of pols, artists, muses, and magicians who literally and figuratively jumped, fully dressed, into party swimming pools up and down the length of the land. Those whose patterns circulated in space around Alice Elizabeth gave her quite a show, to her modest satisfaction.

In a farewell on an early Sunday morning Alice Elizabeth lost her balance at her apartment and did a face-plant at her doorstep as this author was leaving for the airport to go north to the Rockies. Her nose bled, but the indignity and bruises that would turn to black eyes were the worst of it. Dr. Galo took her into the ER for treatment.

In ensuing weeks a consensus developed in our family that Elizabeth should be packed up and moved to Helotes, TX, which was near her grandson-in-law's medical school near San Antonio. The arrangement lasted only a few weeks or maybe a few months until the quartet of small great-grandchildren and the pressure to cooperate with the host family's routine and house rules put far too many limits on Great-grandmother's need of independence in a place far north of *The Laredo Morning Times* and all the pals that she had to leave behind. She felt isolated, and this woman was a social lion in her own mind, past her age of 90.

Death in San Antonio, TX. July 15, 2007

Elizabeth's move from Laredo, to Helotes, TX, was under agreement with her granddaughter, Virginia S. Lynn, whereby the Lynn family took Grandmother into their home. She was then ambulatory and of sound mind to all intents and purposes. There has been brief mention of issues that arose that led to Grandmother's move to The Meadows, an Assisted Living facility on Babcock Rd. in San Antonio

In late 2006 her son and daughter-in-law made one of their thrice-yearly air flights to look in on Elizabeth, always spending a long weekend and at least one or two weekdays, occupied with visits to Grandmother's dentist or the cardiologist who had become her primary care physician. By periodic visits the author was able to keep tabs on Elizabeth's health and cognitive state, enjoying also the company of the Lynn family for lunch or dinner at The Meadows dining facility, which was excellent. A few years of these personal visits to Elizabeth ran by pleasantly until the end of 2006. They facilitated the author's enjoyment of the four grandchildren Virginia Elizabeth Lynn brought into this world during their toddler to early kindergarten years in Helotes.

We made three additional trips in 2007, flying from Colorado Springs or Denver directly to Dallas or San Antonio, because Grandmother's ability to care for herself and continue in charge of her affairs declined. We had several calls a week with Elizabeth or the staff at The Meadows. But in March 2007 Elizabeth herself made plans to enter the skilled nursing facility connected to the main building Meadows for her care. A late springtime visit showed more rapid decline, and the availability of hospice care was explored and arranged for. Even sixty days or so before her death in hospice, she continued to give consent for her treatment. The author and the family were kept very much "in the loop" of decision-making with staff who administered daily care. The prognosis was irreversible decline in cardiac health. On Sunday July 15 hospice contacted us in Colorado to report she had died. Her death instructions were observed, and the arrangements made for burial of her ashes in a grave that had first been opened in May 1944, for burial of Norman W.A. Sorrell at the city cemetery (Masonic section) in Laredo.

This chapter about Alice Elizabeth Nye's decline and death is followed in Appendix 2, which is the obituary that had been lovingly prepared by people at the *Laredo Morning Times*. Appendix 2 is an account of Elizabeth's memorial service at Christ Church parish in Laredo, Texas, on Saturday, July 28, 2007.

EPILOGUE

This is defined by Webster's *New World College Dictionary, 3rd Edition* as "a closing added to . . . novel, play, etc., providing further content, interpretation, or information." Also, a short poem spoken to the audience by an actor at the end of a play.

Under "Recollection of A. P. Nye by Elizabeth Nye" . . . which was written to this author (i.e., one of the very minor characters in the foregoing piece) between 1990 and 2005, there is this quoted material when my mother was responding to my own unhappiness with the changes, slings, and arrows of my own life in about the sixtieth year of life:

"Dear Son, in every family there seems to be some tragedy. Reading about depression, I am dismayed and saddened that one with so much talent and good gifts should suffer from it.

"Let me look back on my youth: *I remember my father as a shadowy figure who lived at the Hamilton Hotel and came down to see us and we said goodbye at our wrought iron gate, we three children in our blue and white checked aprons. I remember his taking us out to Ft. McKintosh to view the retreat when the flag came down and . . . I remember seeing some brightly rouged women in picture hats with plumes who waved gaily at him. I asked 'who are they?' He said 'a bunch of peaches.'* Probably some of the prostitutes he patronized.

"My mother said he was ill because of a disease (syphilis), and in 1918 or thereabouts he was taken away to the hospital. We were brought up not to think about him. We rather considered that he was dead. I never saw him again. Uncle Jack told me that when he went to the hospital, they told him it was best to stay away because he grew worse if visited.

"Vaguely, and if this was a memory of a dream, in our old farm house down by the river, I remember our mother tried to herd us children back, she in her wheelchair, as there was blood on the floor and a girl named Fora and some men, perhaps two. It is so unclear that I don't know if it were a dream or reality. In my later years, I have often thought when I say my prayers.

"I feel this neglect was the largest sin of my life. You know, when we are young, we are cowards; it is only when we grow older that we achieve a kind of courage.

"... I think that both of us must show that we can take it, not matter what. Well, Lupe is here tonight. Tomorrow I buy groceries and we clean house and go to the store and the beauty shop, because keeping one's appearance is part of the good fight.

"Do you mind my sharing a bit of my history and thoughts with you? The time will come when there will be no communication. As in Macbeth, 'after life's fitful fever he sleeps well.'

"Johnnie Murphy was having us to bridge, but she grew ill, and I am sure she is not long for this world. I went to see Bessie (Lindheim) for a while and shared a bit of my thoughts with her. . . . While Bess is petite and pretty, at least she once was, the granddaughter is very tall . . . nothing like her grandmother, but delightful person nevertheless.

"I have already written a little column for Herreras paper. Somehow I am happier at the typewriter, putting words down.
— Love, Mom."

She gave me advice that "both of us must show we can take it no matter what," followed by her comment quoting Shakespeare's *Macbeth*: "the time will come when there is no communication." As in *Macbeth*, "*after life's fitful fever he sleeps well.*" So, now we see allegorically her life (and that part of mine entwined with hers) may have been a "fitful fever." He sleeps well—"he" being the ones who have tossed, turned in a feverish sleep only approximating true rest. He who sleeps well—after life and fruitfulness—gains by the sleep of our final, permanent slumber which Elizabeth held ever before her in her ninety-plus years and which, the truth be told, each of us holds before us at the moment of your reading this. She believed soulfully in *rest being your reward and expectation.*

Therefore, friends, what all of the Nye lives entailed through the ages—now numbering about 1,200-plus years since the duel in Tudse, Denmark, and the sack of Lindisfarne by the Norse—comes down just simply to this: A not-fitful rest, real eternal respite in the arms of the faith of those who flowed out of Genesis.

Is that all there is, you may ask, now? Yes, my friends and readers. Yes to Nye. Yes to other clans. We gain peace by a final, permanent slumber—and then we have *the poetry*! It remains, perhaps forever.

ACKNOWLEDGMENTS

I must give credit to persons who contributed inspiration and guidance to me in the ideas, work, editorial effort, for "She Roared in Classroom 250" in my authorship of the manuscript and publication:

First to Raymond M. Keck, III, President of Texas A&M University, at Laredo, Texas, a gifted organist who facilitated Sunday worship at Christ Church, Episcopal, Laredo, where he saw Elizabeth Sorrell at church functions and during Sunday Eucharists, regularly attended by Ms. Sorrell until her move to Helotes, Tx, in 2005. He suggested a college or University Publisher may be on the list of possible publishers of a print version of this book.

Second, a many years-long professional connection of Alice Elizabeth Nye with the Laredo Morning Times was fostered by Mr. Bill Green, Publisher of the Laredo Morning Times, to Alice Elizabeth Nye Sorrell for at least three decades before 2007. His encouragement of Ms. Sorrell by employing her and by accepting her social columns and news stories submitted to the Times for many years is deeply appreciated now as she also deeply appreciated it during her life.

Third, and foremost for his supportive professional relationship with his former English teacher, we thank Mr. Odilon Arambula, (now deceased) for his professional friendship to our family, from the fifties through Alice Elizabeth's retirement years after 1980, to 2007. He was one life friend and student of Elizabeth, without whose friendship this story would never have been envisioned. Magdalena Zavala, now a resident of Taylor, Texas, her hometown, eighties was an intimate friend of Ms. Sorrell after her retirement from teaching. There are dozens of persons in Laredo who, over Elizabeth's teaching and writing life, are due credit for a similar support-friendship to her.

Thanks also to Ms. Sheila Slaughter-Glassford, a near contemporary in age to the author, a lifelong member of Christ Church Episcopal, and daughter of an esteemed family who figured socially and personally in the lives of Elizabeth and her family for about eight decades.

In the State of Colorado, in Greeley, and in Colorado Springs, these persons and entities were instrumental in bringing this story to publication by various substantive services or skill sets:

- Ms. Catherine Carrithers—for her after hours work in desktop publishing transcription and files management for the author.

- Mr. Stephen Adams—as copy and style editor for this book in 2019, who worked on site and at home, in assembling draft texts and who advised on layout and graphics insertions prior to assembly of the total manuscript at its publication, bringing a background including journalism career at the Cleveland Plain Dealer.

- Mr. Don Kallaus, skilled book designer for Colorado authors, who, with his Rhyolite Press, stepped into the burden of being publisher of this book, and without whose inspired advice this book would never have reached publication.

- Ms. Myrene L. Hoge, the author's spouse, who financed the research, travel and years-long efforts in her household to produce this book and who made every effort to keep the author "on track", moving forward and whose forbearance in many travails since 2014 made this publication possible.

- C. Daniel Miller, PhD., the principal of Integrated Writer Services, LLC, dba "The Copyright Detective" of Greeley, Co., our advisor and agent for copyright permission sought for publication of *She Roared in classroom 250*.

APPENDICES

- Laredo Morning Times newspaper article honoring Journalist
- The Scholarship Fiesta photographs
- Laredo Morning Times Alice Elizabeth obituary
- Interpretation of Courtship letter of page 41
- Transcription of Laredo Morning Times article on page 70

Laredo Morning Times

A City Under Seven Flags
The Gateway To Mexico

Wednesday Dec. 8, 1993

Appendix 1

ALL SMILES: Laredo Morning Times Publisher Bill Green, Society Columnist, Elizabeth Sorrell and LISD Superintendent Vidal Trevino share a laugh during a press conference at the new LISD Magnet School Tuesday.

Times staff photo by MAGDALENA ZAVALA

Hearst Corp., Times honor journalist with scholarship

By SHARON SIMONSON
Times staff writer

Long-time Laredo educator and journalist Elizabeth Sorrell was honored Tuesday with the establishment of a new scholarship fund in her name to benefit communications graduates of LISD's new magnet school.

Laredo Morning Times Publisher Bill Green told a crowd of Laredo Independent School District administrators, instructors and magnet school students that the Hearst Corp. hoped to "prime the pump" with a $10,000 donation to start the fund.

The school district and the newspaper hope to add another $15,000 to the scholarship with a Jan. 14 dinner in Sorrell's honor. The banquet will be sponsored by the Union National Bank and the Laredo National Bank.

"I've had guardian angels — many, many of them," Sorrell said of her life, which included 62 years as a teacher and a reporter. "This little scholarship will be like a guardian angel for these students long, long after I am gone. I do, thank you."

Sorrell's professional career in communications began while she was still in high school at the Laredo Morning Times where she helped write sports news. She attended Rice University, where she graduated, later earning a master's degree in English at the University of Texas at Austin, she said.

As an LISD English teacher between 1931 and 1979, she taught the district's existing superintendent Vidal Treviño.

During her LISD career, Sorrell also taught journalism and helped put out the school's newspaper, the Martin Journal, and yearbook, La Pitahaya, she said.

She also worked for 16 years at the South Texas Citizen.

The brief Tuesday ceremony was held
(See *HONOR Page 16A)

*Honor

(Continued from Page 1A)
at LISD's newly renovated Performing Arts Building at 1702 Victoria. The building houses music and dance classes and is one of four that make up the new LISD magnet school complex, the Vidal M. Treviño School of Communications and Fine Arts.

Five students of the new school spoke eloquently of their experience there. "Being in the magnet school makes me feel special," said Hugo Hernandez, an LISD senior.

"The magnet school is responsible for my educational growth," said Elke Simmons, also an LISD senior. Simmons is now working as an intern at the Laredo Morning Times.

The scholarship should be a start toward allowing Laredo publishers and broadcasters to begin hiring more local talent, said Cynthia M. Ramirez, dean of communications at the new school.

Hiring local journalists at the Laredo Morning Times traditionally has been a challenge, Green acknowledged.

Green said he hoped Tuesday's gesture would be just a first and that in time "others will step forward to establish scholarships" for students in different disciplines.

Laredo Morning Times article about the establishment of a scholarship in honor of Alice Elizabeth to be announced at the civic center event Jan. 14, 1994.

THE SCHOLARSHIP FIESTA

Alice Elizabeth Sorrell and son, Sterling, at the Civic Center fundraising banquet for the Elizabeth Sorrell Communications Scholarship.

Armando Villareal, CPA, left, and grandaughter Virginia Lynn, right, with Alice Elizabeth.

Color guard and orchestra at the Civic Center banquet honoring Alice Elizabeth.

Alice Elizabeth beside her five-tier cake donated for the Scholarship fundraiser.

Friends recall beloved teacher

By CHRISTINA ROSALES
LAREDO MORNING TIMES

A memorial service fit for a Tiger, writer, teacher and a beloved Laredoan, left family, friends, students and community members teary-eyed as they remembered Elizabeth Nye Sorrell.

Sorrell died on July 15, 2007. She was 98.

The memorial service was held on Saturday at 10 a.m. at Christ Church Episcopal on Lane Street.

Poetry was read and her son, Sterling Sorrell, and others shared memories.

Guests exiting the church were greeted by a cheerful tune. The Martin High School Band, in bright red shirts, played the school's fight song and alma mater.

"Oh, I couldn't stop crying when I heard them playing," said Naomi Nye, a friend of Sorrell.

Photo by Theresa Scarbrough | Laredo Morning Times
Family and friends attended Elizabeth Nye Sorrell's memorial services at Christ Church Episcopal Saturday morning.

"She would have been so proud to hear that. She was hugely proud of being a teacher at Martin. She was a Tiger all the way."

During the service, a poem was read by Nye, the same poem honoring Sorrell on her 97th birthday. The poem, titled "When Elizabeth Says A Poem," described Sorrell's love of words and cited words of writers that she lived by.

"One of my first memories of Elizabeth is when I was a teenager at parties," said Ray Keck III, president of Texas A&M International University. "She would excite everyone that came into the place about their food and even their dresses, then she would frame it all with Shakespeare."

One of the most remembered things about Sorrell, Nye said, was her passion for knowledge.

"I would tell my son, he's about 21, that Elizabeth was 98," she said. "But she had the same curiosity as his friends had."

Nye said she teased Sorrell about her need to know everything about everyone.

"When she was at Meadows (assisted living), she had been

See SORRELL | PAGE 12A

there a month and knew everyone's name and life story," Nye said.

What many students remember about Sorrell is her ability to inspire them, Magdalena Zavala said.

While she was never a student of Sorrell's at Martin, Sorrell inspired Zavala.

After a job interview with The Laredo Morning Times, Zavala, a photojournalist, had no place to live and was about to begin working at the paper.

"She invited me to stay with her the very first night of my interview," Zavala said. "It was a match made in heaven and we were instant friends."

Zavala said she admired Sorrell's determination to get a story. Zavala lived with Sorrell for one year.

"It was the happiest time of my life living with her and living in Laredo."

The photojournalist is now a journalism teacher.

"I followed her lead," she said. "I was definitely inspired by her. I guess at some levels she wanted me to pass on to others what I learned."

Sorrell taught many of this generation's teachers in Laredo.

"She was a teacher of teachers," Keck said. "She showed us the impact teachers can have."

John Snyder, a student in Sorrell's class in 1964, said he remembers her enthusiasm for teaching.

"She never complained about anything," Snyder said. "Life, or work, she never wanted you to complain (about) either. She never forced you to be happy, but just by the way she was, she convinced you to be happy."

Nye said Sorrell believed the best in youth and did not like

Courtesy photo by Magdalena Zavala
Elizabeth Sorrell smiles after stopping in at a social event at the Tack Room in this undated photo. Sorrell was remembered fondly at a memorial service Saturday.

people to talk down to teenagers or say anything bad about them.

"She loved the youth," Nye said. "Even after 40 years of teaching, she still believed they were all good."

Nye said she has met Sorrell's former students in Dallas and San Antonio.

"She made an impression on people through the decades," Nye said. "I'll go to places like San Antonio or Dallas, and I ask people from Laredo if they knew her. And they'll say: 'Oh, she was my teacher, the best teacher I ever had.'"

Even after Sorrell moved out of Laredo, she kept in touch with students, friends and her church.

"I used to bring her to church every Sunday," said Jenny Monteith, a parishioner of Christ Church Episcopal for 20 years. "When she left, I sent her programs and let her know what was going on."

Upon the ending of the service, Monteith said she had not "thought to send Elizabeth a program.

"Then I realized I would never send her a program again," she said. "She was a beautiful person."

Sorrell began her career at the Laredo Morning Times while she was in high school and then became an English teacher and yearbook sponsor at her alma mater, Martin High, for 40 years.

Sorrell also wrote a society column for the Laredo Morning Times. She continued writing on deadline, even during her assisted-living years, for LareDos.

Her correspondence with friends, students and even reporters and columnists never faded, even as her handwriting faltered with age, her students said.

Keck said he plans to create the Elizabeth Nye Sorrell Archives at TAMIU to feature the letters and articles she wrote and pictures of her.

"We hope people come forward with things like this so they can be preserved," he said.

In a letter Sorrell sent to Zavala, Sorrell wrote that during a person's being, they are like a supernova.

"She said that we don't ever leave the earth," Zavala said at the memorial service. "We become stars."

(Christina Rosales can be reached through e-mail at crosales@lmtonline.com)

The interpretation of the Courtship letter from page 41:

A handwritten letter of Abel Pirce Nye, writing from the Nye Farm site, north of Laredo, Texas, to his fiancee, Frances McCluskey, at her family's home at Galveston, Texas:

Nye, Aug I, 1906

My Dear Sweet Heart.
Your most welcome letter received with full arms. I am sorry you have had such a headache. I am afraid you work too much. I don't want you to work so much. Pa Pa is after me every day to marry you. I tell him I will have to wait tell you says so. Sweet heart you cant marry me too soon. You don't have to work so hard to fix. I am building a cistern now and the carpenter is working on the house. We had a little shower Here today. And it is cooler. I guess Jack and Inez are having a big time fishing. Sweet heart another reason I want you too marry in August is about the 28 of August I will have to plant cabbage seed and the same time in October I will be planting onion seed I wish I could see you if only for a few minutes maybe you think I wouldnt have lots off kisses lots too With Love too the folks and plenty off love & kisses for you your own boy Pierce Nye.

Here are interprative comments regarding this courtship letter made prior to the wedding and settling-in of Able and Francis on the Nye farmstead located at "Nye Station" a few miles northwest of Laredo Texas:

By the end of 1906, Capt. Thomas C. Nye had settled in Laredo, occupying the house at 1706 Farragut Street while the several Nye sons were working on the farm a few miles north.

A.P. Nye calls his fiancee "Sweetheart". He is responding to a letter from Frances (also called "Faye') written to him in July. He states concern for Faye's headache in Galveston.

"Pa Pa", Abel Pierces' father, saw his sons frequently, in close contact around the farm. A.P reports his father, ? ? ? is after him to go and marry the girl Faye, in Galveston, after which he would bring her home to the Laredo farm. Perhaps the house to which A.P referred midway through his letter is the farmhouse which A.P, and his bride would adopt as their dwelling.

After A.P. and Frances settled in as marrieds, on February 4, 1909, Alice Elizabeth Nye was born on the farm. She appears in the foreground of the photo made on the farm, where she appeared to be a toddler of perhaps 2 years of age.[See picture page 43].

After mention of the rain, A. P. comments on of Jack, the youngest son of Capt. Nye, and Inez, who was at that time the unmarried older sister of Faye. The circumstances suggest that Jack Nye was then visiting Galveston, and Inez (older sister of Faye), was conducting Jack on day trips to the Galveston beaches or docks for fishing.

The timing of the marriage of A.P and Faye is put in context to times near at hand when A.P would be in the fields, supervising the planting of cabbage and, later in the fall, onions, from seed— as if to suggest the marriage and settling in on the farm, while planting crops would have limited the time Abel could be available to his bride.

As suitor for Faye's hand, A. P. said he "wishes he could see Faye even if for only a few minutes time". He signed off as "your own boy Pierce " We think the couple were married on or about,1906, not long after the love letter was delivered to Frances McCluskey.

Transcription of the Laredo Morning Times article on page 70:

A LAREDO LEGEND NAMED ELIZABETH SORRELL

For good reason, an off-the-cuff comment imade by the county at last week's commissioners meeting, relit our interest in one of those occasional letters we get from a grand lady living in a retirement home in San Antonio.

It's one of these hand-written letters, done in lead pencil, that other people here are fortunate to get from a jewel of a human being, dear Elizabeth Sorrell.

We're still looking for that file where we stored Liz Sorrell's words of wisdom, but we remember well what she was telling us.

In the opening line, she started by mentioning. "my dear friend Josephine Brand," crediting Mrs. (Joe) Brand for sending her clips of Laredo Morning Times articles. One of these recent pieces mentioned Louis J. Christen, someone Mrs. Sorrell knew well. Christen was some smart fellow: an onion farmer who went on to become a city alderman, city mayor and school superintendent. That middle school on Park is named after the man.

MRS. SORRELL TELLS HOW the man built his home with a roof to facilitate the flow of snow (rain) from the roof, In the body of the letter, she drew something that looked like the structure she was describing, She penciled some compliments and signed off with an exclamatory about her 97th birthday. At a recent celebration function, Mrs. Sorrell was the topic of a conversation with Jenny Reed.

"Elizabeth is turning 97. She's as sharp as ever and is still writing," Jenny said.

So whats the point on the county judge's comment on the appointment of two members to the county historical commission? None whatsoever. The comments were benign, and perhaps complimentary in light of the storm to come over the election results. 'To quote County Judge Louis

H. Brunt himself, he's not a bad guy. It's a public officials natural reaction to public criticism. He has a lot of company in this town.

Despite the silence of the lame ducks at the podium and the visitors, we had a good laugh. It was one of the finest compliments paid this writer by an elected official at a public meeting (and Public Access).

We reflected on Mrs. Sorrell's letter and the events surrounding her early newspaper experiences with the Times many years (79) ago when she was a senior at old Laredo High School We understood it as an expression of students petting on public officials' backs, urging them to do something about their schools. It got results.

Researching material by Times writers from other times, particularly Jim Falvella and Star Castillo, we rediscovered Mrs. Sorrell in her roles, first as reporter and assistant editor of the school paper, and then editor her senior year (1927).

We first heard stories at Martin High School, where she taught for decades. Her strange accounts of Tiger football games, getting 10 cents an inch, apparently caught the attention of the editor, William Prescott Allen.

That year, the Times took an Elizabeth Nye-bylined article and published it. She called for a change in colors of the Tiger football team uniforms, It became the subject of a school student assembly.

Thereafter, the newspaper published another article by Miss Nye, an essay on the need to expand and improve school curriculum, listing courses In the language arts (writing and journalism), sciences, social studies, economics, business, vocational training, physical education, a Library, etc.

The PRINCIPAL took notice. The superintendent took notice. The school board took notice and heard from the advocates who agreed with what the young woman detailed in the essay. It planted the seeds that meant, within the next decade, Laredo would have a brand-new, state-of-the-art high school—Raymond and Tirza Martin High School.

That summer of 1927, the Times' editor, Allen, soon to acquire the paper from H.E. Hanway, hired her as a reporter at $10 a week. There's nothing in print to suggest that someone accused her of getting on anyone's back. It did, however, stir community interest, and within the decade Laredo had voted bonds to match federal funding for the new high school.

People out of the Texas Education Agency called the school one of the finest buildings in Texas at the time. When the school graduated its first class and produced its first yearbook (La Pitahaya, 1937), the dedication went to Elizabeth Nye Sorrell.

We appreciate her because, like so many teachers from the old school, she's not shy about expressing pride in her former students who made something of themselves. These young men and women represented a reflection of the quality teaching they got from her and others.

MRS. SORRELL USED TO MAKE fun, telling people that we never gave her any compliments during her tenure at the Times. It was really her harmless way of complaining about the editor. At a retirement dinner before an overflowing crowd at the civic center, a former student who became a school superintendent, Vidal M. Trevino, introduced her.

She walked to the podium and, among other things, told the full house, "You Know, Odie never pays me compliments. But that's all right. He always calls me 'girl.'"

While researching material on Falvella and Eduardo Alvarez del Castillo (Star Castillo) in connection with the newspaper's 125th anniversary, we retrieved images of her early ties with the newspaper. We learned from a 1926 Old Laredo High School yearbook where a brilliant high school junior named Elizabeth Nye was writer and assistant editor for the school paper.

Decades later she shared her recollections of a high school principal (Teo Seyfried) who sponsored the school paper and was her first mentor. She became the school newspaper's editor her senior year and got a job covering football games for the Laredo 'Nmes. The paper did not have a sports editor on staff.

SHE REPORTED FROM information she gathered from the players on the bench. Mrs. Sorrell, like the schoolgirls of that era, didn't know the science of a game in which boys would knock themselves senseless trying to push a pigskin ball across the goal line for a score.

They played with limited gear for protection. The object was to push a pigskin ball across the goal line to score six points. Some wore helmets and others did not. The fellows were so rawboned and so tough that they went undefeated and unscored on that year (1927). They were district champions. By that year, the Times had already been sold by then-owner-publisher Justo S. Penn to a fellow from Casper, Wyo., named H.B. Hanway.

Mrs. Sorrell's compensation was 10 cents an inch.

Hanway is part of a nutty chapter in the history of the Laredo Morning Times. Penn had run the newspaper since 1901 after the death of his father, James Saunders Penn, who started the paper. While running the Times, Penn served an abbreviated term in the Texas Legislature, having been appointed to the unexpired term of Charles C. Pierce in 1910.

Penn did his civic duty and resumed management of the newspaper until he turned it over to Hanway in 1926.

That 1927 summer, the Times had Mrs. Sorrell reporting on civic clubs, sporting events and other stuff, including obituaries. The newspaper plant was in a building shared with H.L. Jackson Funcral Home on Farragut. The newspaper plant later was moved to a location on Matamoros.

It would have been great to have had Mrs. Sorrell at the recent LULAC-sponsored Laredo International Latin Hall of Fame banquet. Among the inductees were the members of that 1927 Old High district championship team coached by Shirley DaCamara. The lone survivor of that team is Radcliffe (Radz) Killam.

Shirley DaCamara's daughter, Prissy, represented her late father and the 1927 team at the head table. The football field at Martin High is named after her dad. Mrs. Sorrell taught Prissy at Martin High.

Our calendar has several marks for traveling to San Antonio one of these days. This time we're going to find the place (The Meadows) to continue the conversation. There must be hundreds (make that thousands) in Laredo who have run into her here, there, everywhere. Don't be surprised if you are asked, "Did I teach you?" She probably will want to know if you're important.

In our album of memories, Elizabeth Nye Sorrell is important. She will always be important to the hundreds and thousands whose lives she touched in and out of the classroom.

She started teaching language arts (English), putting emphasis on English literature. She was the town's expert on Shakespeare. She sponsored the yearbook for years, and in her late teaching years she taught journalism and sponsored The Journal, She covered women's news (socials) for years for the Times, and to this day she contributes regularly to Larado's and this newspaper's Art of Living section.

We don't have a recollection of ever greeting Mrs. Sorrell in any press box at Shirley Field. She is a real Tiger Legend. Her first and only press box was the team bench.

Belated happy birthday, Girl.

Notes/Bibliography

1. L. Bert Nye, *A Genealogy of American Nyes of English Origin, Vol. I*, (East Sandwich, MA, The Nye Family of America Association, 1977), 21.

2. Robert McCrum, William Cran, Robert MacNeil, *The Story of English*, (New York, Viking Penguin, Inc., 1986), 115.

3. Winston Churchill, *A History of the English Speaking Peoples Vol. 2*, (New York, Dodd, Mead & Co., 1956), 171.

4. When, that is, she became self-conscious or capable of self-definition as a child or young adult.

5. It was founded in 1630, according to Wikipedia.

6. "The Desolate Wilderness," *The Wall Street Journal*, 11/23/2011.

7. Larry McMurtry, *Lonesome Dove*, (New York, Simon & Schuster, 1985). 30.

8. Tom Miller, *On the Border*, (New York, Harper & Rowe Publishers, Inc., 1981), 60-62.

www.ingramcontent.com/pod-product-compliance
Lightning Source LLC
Chambersburg PA
CBHW060940170426
43195CB00023B/2982